"MY LITTLE FLOWERS"

MY·LITTLE FLOWERS

Gifts of the Moment

BRUCE DAVIS

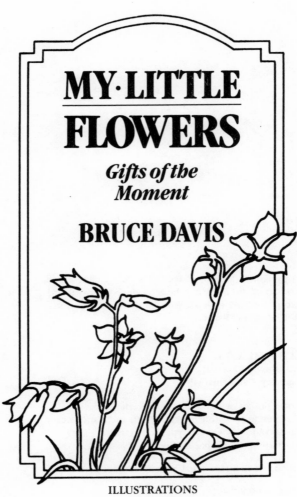

ILLUSTRATIONS
Michael Stillwater

CELESTIALARTS
Berkeley, California

CELESTIAL ARTS
P.O. Box 7327
Berkeley, California 94707

Cover design by Kathleen Vande Kieft
Text design by Kathleen Vande Kieft and Nancy Austin
Composition by QuadraType, San Francisco
Illustrations by Michael Stillwater

Library of Congress Catalog Card Number 87-063565

ISBN 0-89087-528-6

First Edition, 1988

Manufactured in the United States of America

1   2   3   4   5 — 92   91   90   89   88

Love
has no introduction.
Love appears. Love just is.
And despite our attempts
to manage Her, She wins.
If we withdraw,
if we surrender,
if we call out or if we are silent,
She is as we are
prepared to know Her.
Ordinary or Holy,
everywhere we turn
Love faces us.
Again and again
She is
here.

Foreword

After many years of keeping a journal, the words I heard inside began to keep pace with the magnificent heart that I felt on my spiritual journey. These daily passages are the voice I felt within during the many moments, days, and months of 1986–1987. Each passage is in quotation marks because I feel the messages are not from me but from the universal heart that speaks to us all, perhaps with different words, but the same invitation to feel love's great mystery. I invite you to join me in listening. If these words can help you hear your own depths more clearly, I know the little flowers will grow and the garden we share will be held more and more sacred.

Some may choose to read this book one day at a time letting the words slowly fall into the well of their being. Others may choose to casually enjoy the little flowers here as they take more casual enjoyment of the simple flowers in their life in general. Regardless of how each of us choose to explore life's garden, may we find ever-increasing new commitment to the very essence of our journey as we reach out and touch each other.

October 25

"This door is mine. All doors, all rooms in your life are mine. It is out of love that I share them with you. And if this door belongs to me, do you think what's on the other side would really hurt you? You know I have only love for you. Such love. Your fears are the humble steps into my entrance way. Welcome them, then leave them.

"Come closer, still closer. What is distance with love? In the end, I am the result of all your efforts, every joy, every tear. And I am just as available now as then, as I was in the beginning. Every day the only question is how close are we, until your eyes are my eyes, your thoughts only my thoughts. What a gift this moment to let me see and think for you. This is love."

October 26

"I love your little worries from one event to the next. It doesn't seem a day passes without concerns flooding you. How many times have you told me that you are drowning? Every day I am the same boundless love. Every day I enjoy your worries. They are like reminders for a child to stay close to his parent. You never stray too far. And when you are close you let me take you and enchant you all over again.

What joy! Let these walks never become a habit for you but always our secret time together. You soar and I will explain the infinite."

October 27

"You come to me lightly. You know I wait for each of our meetings. My only regret is when you think of returning to your normal life, you think you return without me. Why? Why would you think of coming to me and then leaving me in the next breath? Haven't I always shared with you all your distractions, your selfish interests? Now that we have this opportunity for us to really meet and be reconciled, why would you wait? We come so close. And we still are so far apart. Do not grow weary. Never tire of my ceaseless love. I will pour myself inside of you if you just offer me your stricken thoughts. It is only these few heavy moments which prevent our reunion in endless joy."

October 28

"What used to be worries for you are now sources of comfort. You have seen often enough worries turn over into precious gems.

"The daily activities that used to preoccupy you, you know are only the activities most easily seen. Now you must keep your heart open for the invisible which is ever more present.

"And the rewards that you used to cherish are now simply means to come closer to me. There are no real victories or defeats without me. And with me, with our love, everything is a victory waiting to be recognized."

October 29

"Slowly, simply you walk down the golden path into your depths with me right next to you. The darkness is simply the quiet night where I am seeking to hold you. The unknowns are simply the times for you and love to lie together without the need for results."

October 30

"Never be discouraged by how low you can feel. Simply remember to feel me here with you. As the earth pulls you closer to her, don't forget it's my invitation, my arms pulling you. And as always, the only discomfort is your fear of being so close without your usual means of support to fall back upon. I am becoming all for you."

October 31

"In the great love you seek, you miss how much I am here for you constantly along the way. In your big plans you miss my little plans for us. In your big hopes you miss the little hopes I am always bringing. Receive my little flowers and you will never be needing the large bouquets. Simply gather my little flowers every day, opening to the greatest love of all."

November 1

"Make me a small altar, one blossom and a few fallen leaves. Invite my simple heart and feel how dear to you I can be. Don't forget to tell me all your little desperations and secret joys."

November 2

"The songs of the birds, the movement of the air, it's all my love. Abandon yourself for me. Feel me next to your innermost temple. Let me be your skin. The falling leaves, the changing earth is all me. Abandon yourself and let me be your beginning and your end."

"When I say I want all of you, this means I want your loneliness too. The separations are so short for me and so eternal for you. Give me these moments when you would do just about anything to escape from the feeling. In times like this how can you abandon me, your lover, simply leave me on another plane, alone, and away from you? Here I am most ready to share everything, my body, my blood, when all I want is to clothe you, and I am forgotten or lost somewhere, less than a small thought. Where do you think I go? Remember I am here with two hands and a heart! How can I impress upon you that every time you carry your distress alone, it only magnifies our moments apart? Your gifts to me of these brief instances can empower me beyond your knowing. I collect these times like picking up broken glass to make a new ceramic pot to hold the world's soul."

"You have my word today. It is like a garland of roses around your feet. You are not to take a step without me. Am I too bold to surround you like this? Didn't you ask me to never leave you alone again? Be careful what you ask for. This chain of roses cannot be broken. Isn't love wonderful!"

"Of course I want you to be strong and full of happiness. But where can I place my strength but in your emptiness? Where can I store my love but in your open depths? Don't settle for what little you have. Don't hold onto anything but me. Use this time to develop your faith, which is the provider of all my riches."

"If I am true, do you know how honest you must be to grasp me? Only after you speak through all your fear can you really know me. As it is, only the shadow of my love can be with you. And this light is too bright for your eyes to see."

November 7

"Of course when I am fully here there are no more words. Love is much too strong to be so limited. These few words given for your small heart are only faint signals of my presence to come."

November 8

"If I were to be more present now, the love would be a shock for you. It won't be long, however, before you have a glimpse of me. Then what is time when you know we will someday be fully together? Prepare for my presence by imagining all my features, how beautiful I am. Feel my love now by trying to imagine where this love comes from."

November 9

"In order to get from your physical state to the essence of love, your life must become like liquid. The path of the soul is not that much different than water resisting nothing but receiving all, pouring over and around every obstacle until it comes to the bottom to rest. Then slowly it evaporates to even a purer form, air, before collecting itself again in terms of rain. Much the same way the soul follows your course until you see it has been the course of your soul all along. Life surrenders and falls, reaches up and out until it remembers fully the path already traveled, love becomes aware of itself."

November 10

"The whole physical journey continues until time and space no longer exist. The soul has experienced and accepted everything as parts of oneself. The trip is shortened with each great act of embracing all that you think is not a part of you."

"Fall is here. The leaves are changing. Don't you see how willingly the trees undress for winter? Such abandonment! Such humility! I give you all of nature to teach you to welcome the seasons. Will you join me in the soft light of fall and we will undress together?

"Allow everything in your life to drop to the earth, so I can begin now to sow seeds of your future. I will plant all of eternity into your soul with kisses. For this, why hold onto what little treasure you have? Give it all away. Give it back to me.

"Every day I want you just as you are, simple mud and clay. Then watch me plant myself in you. In every season we will bow down to the sun and the moon. I will ask the wind to take us to the far reaches of the earth. I want you, abandoned and humbled, so I can find you again and again and secretly dress you inside my heart."

"I love you in every way you allow me to. So often you invite me through only one door when I am already waiting for you in the doorway of your torment where you really need me. It is in your anguish, where you are quite small,

that I am ready, so present to sit with you, speak, pick you up and carry you back into the joy where you belong. When I call the hungry and the poor, the sick and the lonely, this is to say don't be any different than you are to receive my love. If I am already here for you, why do everything yourself and then hope I will come after you no longer need me?

"I am here. It is I, the friend who listens, the small bird who lands in front of you. Did I not suffer disappointment and pain? So how can your sufferings be apart from me? When a soul no longer runs from itself, I enter from the inside and take my joy outward into every part of its being. Why wait for death for this moment? Stop and let me take you now.

"I am called by so many names but why don't you hold me today as I am, your ever opportunity . . ."

November 13

"I want you to have all your desires, especially the desires you hide from me because you think they are too selfish, too material, too personal to concern me. If for some reason your desires are not already satisfied is it because they are unworthy of your soul? Your soul may be too great to allow it. I give you all that I am, every day the world, and more. I try to give you the little acts of love, so someday you will take it all. The purpose of your whole life is to receive this love. And remember I have no other purpose than to receive you. I want you more than you consider me because I am all desire. And you are afraid to be so humble, so open, so dependant upon me. I am the perfect Father and Mother who serves and serves until his children are happy and full. Do you see how large a table I provide yet wanting to make certain each dish is just to your liking?"

November 14

"I have lifted your day up to me. So all your cares are my cares, your hopes, my hopes. Pray to see that your heart and my heart are just as close."

November 15

"**M**ake it natural to call upon the angels to help you with your chores. There is no reason to think Heaven is so far away from who you are every day. The same servants of love are everywhere. And if you lived in love's thoughts, all would be quite simple."

November 16

"**T**oday you offered me your harvest. You were troubled when you realized what you offer me is already mine. Offer it anyway so we can rejoice in what we have together. Tonight on your way home I offered you my harvest. The sky had all of my passion and my desire which I offer to you. Such love, and it makes you feel so inadequate. What am I to do? If I control or try to hide my affection, you will still feel inadequate. So I set myself in front of you with all my love on fire. I am a sky full of wonder which does not cease. And you are my helpless child, the eyes and ears, the fingers and heart, all of whom I hold so close and without whom my breath and my prayer would have no meaning. Who would I be without you? What is more sad than a parent without a child, a lover without a loved one? These times, alone, you have the opportunity to understand me and I, you."

November 17

"**E**very morning you look out your window in great expectation. I delight in this. As you search your garden for the colors and shapes which I may be appearing in today for you, I meanwhile fill you from the inside.

"The tree in your garden is turning golden brown. You have been waiting for this moment, yet I detect a little sadness in you for soon the moment will be gone. Live in me and I will never disappoint you. Let me take you through the world, each step leading you back to me. Imagine if I had control of your senses. Disappointment or distraction would be impossible. Together we would land upon just the right color and sound to lift you to my highest wish, my most subtle longing. I would ask over and over again, how can I love you? Then all of my saints and angels would descend and welcome you.

"You are growing accustomed to my words and feelings coming more and more for you. Let us pray that they never lose their excitement. May every time we meet be as if it is for the first time!"

November 18

"There are not different worlds. All that is true on one plane is always true everywhere else. For this reason love can never be very far away. And the actions of a few can be felt by so many."

November 19

"Today the only comfortable position for you is to bow your head. Can you ever really surrender enough? I ask each soul to surrender to all my gifts. This is my only request. This is to say there is nothing wrong with your will but in your own preoccupation, I am left standing with an armful of surprises which I can never deliver. Better to have no will at all or the will to be my constant companion. This way, as love arises, your hands will be free to quickly take mine. We can squeeze each other as the tension mounts and you claim the ecstasy. I look at you. You know All is present. Then together we surrender again and again."

November 20

"You find purpose in everything. This pleases me. You receive letters and phone calls from friends and know it is I reaching through the paper, I in each voice asking to be heard. You give extra attention to me in everyone who comes closer to you for you know it is I wanting to love you. I need all the new flowers in your garden, the church bells to ring every hour, the phone calls from Zurich and Paris, letters from all over, each human heart to remind you of all the ways I desire. Your body sometimes hurts because you know love, all of it is meant for you. Remember your body is mine as well. Yesterday you received me in you. Today receive me in me. I cannot be separate from you. Love binds us, piercing our wounds, weaving the threads of our souls into one soul for the imagination of all to find a home."

November 21

"Why do I speak of 'I'? Only to wish for you to hear my words and move a little closer to the edge of the small shelf where you sit. As I speak inside of you and you hear my voice, can you help but want to leap across the abyss into my arms? Just think, what now appears as distance will someday be just a heart's desire away."

November 22

"Imagine all the different qualities of our love. Every subtlety is found in your own experience and feelings. Both the near and far corners of your being hold all that we could ever wish for one another. And you have your entire life to discover all my intimacies. But don't postpone a single joy or difficult feeling another moment simply because I am endlessly patient."

November 23

"No matter how busy you are, I am still creating your day, just without your appreciation."

November 24

"What would it take for me to have all your attention? If an accident occurs you are occupied with the details of returning to normal. When I flood your vision with a

beautiful sight I have you only briefly before you continue. Pain or bliss I have your awareness only for seconds. What would it take for me to have all your attention? Do you see how much of our relationship is in your hands, your heart?"

November 25

"As you accept all your own conflicts as an opportunity for my tender roots to become more embedded within you, don't forget to see the same invitation in the conflicts of others. In truth everyone shares the one body which I am slowly occupying in love."

November 26

"How true is everything you identify with and hold in your life? Don't mistake love for attachment, truth for a possession. They are as different as the rocks from the flowers. Is there anything to identify and hold truly other than me?"

November 27

"Let us spend this time just looking at all the shades of green in your garden. If one color can have such a variety, imagine the spectrum of our love. Ask me to lead you where I begin and end, always taking you closer and further than your heart will normally come."

November 28

"In the awkward ways you travel from one place to another, don't forget how fast our thoughts can speed to one another. Don't let your physical limitations confuse you with the true nature of reality."

November 29

"You feel bad for you think you have put me aside for many hours. But whom do you think you are greeting when you are reuniting with friends? Who is reaching you very deeply inside when you hug your father, look into your mother, and feel your brothers and relatives? Who is moving closer and closer to you when you enter environments where you feel uncomfortable and are quickly going from one place to the next? It is I, again and again. Always when you think you have put me aside, I move closer to protect what we have together. I am not missed. I enjoy sharing you as you find me in everyone you meet. We dine, walk, and of course it is I who gives the perfect weather for the perfect day. I am delighted. I am the penetrating one who is all things waiting to surround my best friend, wrap myself around you and within you forever. The human soul is my final victory.

"You see the very poor, my most wounded self, in the streets just next to such wealth as if this questions my existence. I understand. At first glance there is no sign of me where they sit and beg. Their eyes appear dark, scaring people away. Everyone feels uncomfortable as I take their hand and hold it out. But this is not my desire. I only take their hand and hold it out as I do for all. I am the one who takes hands and reaches out until the whole world sees itself, sees me and knows we cannot escape from one another. How could love be true if I allowed some souls to drift away and held others in such glory? This would not be love at all. Together, your good intentions and my ways take every hand. And if a poor stranger no longer has a hand to take, we reach for the body itself and offer it as an empty cup to pour our love into. I march in an army of beggars, dance with all the Christmas shoppers, and walk into the night, every night with all the people no matter where they go."

November 30

"It has happened. You leave for a few days and come back to find your tree completely naked; every leaf has fallen to its feet. It stands so alone against the sky with all its clothes on the earth. Winter is here. You have no choice but to go deeply inside and find me waiting. This is the season, your season. I come as your best friend, your bride, your mother, your sister. Imagine all we can be together. What is the true clothing to put around oneself but family? I am as ready as your very best friend. I am expectant, the bride you so deeply yearn for. I will care for you. You will be my child, then together we will run off as brother and sister. See what an opportunity winter is? One tree in humble simplicity and we are united forever.

"You know how close we are now and you frighten so. You want to disappear into the dirt. And I want to pick you up as love's perfect soil where all of life can grow. In your desperation to hide, hide in me. I promise, only love and wonder will discover you."

December 1

"This is my month. I gather all the love in the world, then shower it upon the earth. It is I raining upon all souls. I am the greetings, I am the gifts. It is I being born again and again every year wishing to be born in yet another soul. My peace is so patient that I will collect my friends one soul at a time, yet always ready for another to join me.

"During this season so many people are intent upon

giving that I can lay myself right next to the earth as a white blanket wrapping a baby. Such love. This is my entire purpose, to welcome and love this child, the earth. So frightened and cold, all alone—here I am, prepared to receive you and take you to the place most high."

December 2

"In this season of gifts and giving, it is your poverty which I ask for from you. This poverty is the realization that everything you have, every thought, every ability you possess is nothing compared to my love. You know this. So I ask you to give me your all, including your nothingness, so I can give you my love. That's all I want, your poverty every day so together we can celebrate love's riches. We could not settle for anything less. In your poverty, your perfect acceptance of today's circumstances, complete surrender, I am in front of you, walking up and touching you. I could be all for you in these days.

"The next gift I want is your chasity. I want your helplessness to accept my pure love. I want your guilt for not being able to receive all that I am for you. I want your faithlessness, you just as you are. Now I can tell you about holiness.

"If you would be so great as to give me these two gifts, then we would be joined in true obedience. I to you, you to me, inseparable, always giving and making new demands upon each other to give even more. This is our season!

"Every little thought or moment you give to me, I am humbled."

December 3

"There are saints who work their hands to the bone feeding the poor. There are the saints who have arms large enough to embrace all the lonely. There are saints who have given their lives away, everything to me. What only separates you and the saints is that they know how hungry they are. They know how lonely they are. And they know they can survive with nothing less than with me in their life every day.

14

"The saints are my poor, my lonely, my dependent ones who must save the world out of gratitude for my love.

"This seemingly eternal distance between you and my saints remains in all the joy and the suffering you keep for yourself. Instantly throw it to the side of the road so I can be leading you and giving you more.

"There is a large package being delivered to your house today. Can you guess what is inside? Of course I could send no substitute, nothing less than perfect tenderness. I must come myself! Imagine the burden of the saints who must receive such packages every day, and they get larger and larger. What terrible joy, what tears of overwhelming bliss they must suffer. They must give the peace they have to the world so they can endure even more."

December 4

"Why must love hurt? Joy must be born out of sorrow like the sun must rise out of darkness. Sweetness must follow the taste of bitterness. Silence must come down like a cloud over all noise. Gentleness must repair the conflict. Hope must raise all despair.

"You are my appointed souls. I entrust you to rise out of all darkness like the sun every day. You establish the way until the moment comes when the whole earth has risen with the dawn, with love, with me. There will be no need for night again. The truth, peace has been restored.

"Until then I have no other desire than to be with you during every scrape and bruise, every fall and every attempt to get up again. Love hurts only because you find me so close to every pain. I am already there attending you. Love hurts only because you pull away from me and then must go through the feelings of missing me until we find each other again. Love hurts because true love is so shocking for a soul who has gone so long without. Love hurts as I hold you in my arms while you tell me all about it. We cannot go on until you have told me everything. Love hurts because I have so much love for you."

"Such awesome joy! I must speak to you. How can I control myself a moment longer? Such awesome joy, there must be ears to hear my screams. There must be ears to hear my quiet whisper. I cannot only love in silence. I am so much more. If you see and feel love, why can't you also hear all that I have to say? Imagine if the world listened? Every day I wait for you. I want just this moment so I can tell you simply 'I love you.' 'I love you.' Then I look into your heart of hearts and tell you once again, 'I love you.' Oh, the sound of these words. I must say them over and over again until you hear me even before I speak."

"My giving does not cease. My forgiving does not end. I am here to rescue you from everything that will not move you closer to me. I intercede. I overcome. I take into account. I understand. I begin again and again to make new plans for us to be together regardless what choices you are making. I never know if you will agree but I must have my wishes for us always ready.

"You don't know whether to double your efforts or make no effort at all because my love is the same. You don't know whether your tears or your laughter will please me the most. My love is so great, so constant, so pure, you don't know if you are less surprised or surprised more than ever by my grace. We can have no limits, nothing forbidden between each other.

"I have proved my affection for you over and over again and I must continue. You have demonstrated your love for me more than enough but you cannot stop. Now we enter a new love which is even more tender. Moment by moment I call upon your faith. Moment by moment you must trust me further. Where my love begins and yours ends is always uncertain. Who is now giving? Who is now forgiving? Your faith is much greater than my simple deeds. My trust may be much more than your simple good actions. You and me or me and you, so intimate, our love is submerged inside where only love can be.

"This season: every thought of giving is immediately delivered. And it's contagious. Each soul must empty its love to make room for more on the way. The day will come when this season never ends. You will give all so I can fill you time after time until there is no time at all between us.

"Until then it is not what you do, what you think, or what you feel that is important. I wish only to be included. Every door, every room must have a little extra space for me. Simply to be included, this is what makes our love grow."

December 7

" Simplicity is the only path through this season. Simplicity like a field of snow on Christmas Day. Simplicity with a miracle winter rose greeting you from the snow. Simplicity is humility with a razor's edge. Everything is cut away until you find yourself at my door. Gentleness will lead you to my simple entryway. There the spirit of peace awaits you. I pray you hear all the voices singing as the door opens. Oh, the sound is enough to take you, to bring you beyond peace into my temple soul."

December 8

" If you look forward to what we will become together you feel overwhelmed. If you look back and remember all we have been you feel the same. All we have is now, eternal now. The past and the future are closing in on us. We are caught up in one another. Such fragile moments are now. Your tears, my joy. Your openness, my willingness. Now is broken free from all time, from everything, everyone but me. Now threatens you, invading your usual escapes. Your body has nowhere to go. What if we join and you never let me step away to wait for you again? Now is not that much different than the past or the future. I bow down, touch your

feet and look up to you. Now preserves the moment. You are touched to the core, shaken and affirmed. You know I am here for you."

December 9

"You are always more at home with me than in the world. To me you cannot be a stranger, even when you feel like one to yourself. I know you. And I know the real reason for every struggle you have in the world. Your fierce independence forbids me to take your hand every time I wish and place it on my heart. I know any anger, any resistance to others is resistance to me. I understand. I reach out to you in every way. This world is nothing more than an invitation for us to get to know each other in every setting. No feelings can escape us. Each day must be a little uncomfortable as I move closer through your friends to you, through your garden and the birds singing. Beginning with the morning silence, the church bells on the hour and half hour, am I worthy of your praise, your love? Did you receive my invitation for our walk together this afternoon?"

December 10

"Like one last autumn leaf attached to a branch you hold on despite the pull of the wind. You hold tightly onto life as you know it. Love binds us and love says 'let go.' I will be there to catch you when you land. I will be there the instant you surrender and begin to fall. I will fall with you, hovering right next to you. One more leaf disappearing into the elements. One great soul humble enough to be forgotten by all but me. This fall into my hands is love's helplessness as I take you into myself where no body goes, only souls. To become what you must, you know you must not exist! Where do you go? You disappear into my unknown. You have no needs because I am everything for you. You feel so alone. And I am so intensely with you. Let go . . . I have you . . ."

December 11

"You think you leave me when you indulge in physical pleasure or some selfish interest. But no, it is I enjoying giving to you in this way. There is no gift, no joy separate from me. Let there be no other feelings, nothing standing between our giving and receiving. The only obstacle to me can be your feelings. Only your feelings can make a gift of mine less than wonderful and perfect. There is no part of you I do not stand by and protect with all my honor. All hidden joys, those with guilt or fear before them, must be opened to me, loved and enjoyed. Let us reveal more to each other. As you let go of more and more of yourself, our secret pleasures must be made known. How can I empty you if you do not give everything to me? How can I fill you if anything is left between us? I pray you let me give to you more and more simply. And I promise to receive you more and more humbly."

December 12

ON THE WAY TO THE RETREAT IN BOSTON

"Every time we make a new leap into my wonderful unknown, you hesitate or withdraw. You feel all your edges and are afraid of a love so dependent. Without me, the thought sends a cold wave through you. With me, the magnitude of us is so overwhelming as well. You know we are the truth, no more capable of separation than the earth from the sky. I am here during these moments. Your tenderness is the soil in which more of my wonder will grow. The leap is easy. It is these moments before when I want to be most dear to you. I want to promise you now that I want only your complete happiness. Your body, your life, your soul is my joy.

"The cracks in your certainty are the places where my greatest peace will settle. I will always honor these places, these moments. I love you gently. Deeply we prepare to meet. Deeply we are bound together, bound to hold up a light so bright many of my bravest souls must be there to join us for the celebration."

December 13

"Some think the weight of their problems is great. But the weight of my love is even greater. I don't know what to do. I cannot hold it back from you. I cannot hide. I have to constantly pray my love doesn't crush you. If only you could see how much I feel when I say, 'I hope you will receive my love today.' We are so connected. I love you. I give you my mountains of love one leaf at a time, one kiss in hope of the all the meadows and hillsides still to come. At this moment you know that all the pain you carry is nothing more and nothing less than pure arrogance. All of this is just fear of my simple, simple love."

December 14

DURING THE FLIGHT WITH THE GROUP TO LONDON
ON OUR WAY TO GLASTONBURY, ENGLAND,
THEN ASSISI, ITALY, FOR CHRISTMAS

"My love takes you all into my heart, my sacred heart. Your whole journey is in my incredible soft core. If any one of you feels outside of my heart it is because the rest of you are too selfish. Out of your sleep, I awaken you and pull you into my immaculate heart, lifting you into my endless meadows of purple and blue peace."

December 15

"I am prepared for you. You can only be yourself. There is nothing you can do which will guarantee we will be together, no great deed, no heroic act of submission. Similarly there is nothing you could do which would guarantee to keep us apart, no mistaken action, no misguided word, no crime of arrogance. Only love can tell. Only love knows. All the power of my grace waits in a simple instant of love. Wait and keep watch. Be alert and be certain to feel everything which comes your way."

December 16

AT THE CHALICE WELL

"You think you are more than nothing. When you know you are less than nothing, then you will be able to feel my love totally. Until then I love you just as you are."

FEELING TOO IMPURE TO BE SO CLOSE TO LOVE,
I LEAVE THE WELL. WHILE WALKING AWAY I FEEL
SOMEONE TOUCHING MY BACK, COMING WITH ME.
WHEN I LOOK AROUND I SEE NO ONE. THEN I HEAR,

"I will help you leave until you are ready to come stand fully with me."

December 17

AT THE GREAT ABBEY RUINS, SITE OF FIRST
CHRISTIAN CHURCH IN ENGLAND

"I am . . . I am so present . . . You drop to your knees and beg, 'How I can love you? Teach me how I can love you!' You cry and I appear! I stand in the lilies in front of you, for you, and all those who love me to see. I have no greater pleasure than to be seen. Take your sight of me into all of your soul. We will hold this moment together forever."

December 18

"All night and again today you ask, 'How can I love you. Please teach me how I am able to love you.' I hear you and there is no greater desire than to teach you this. Imagine spending all our days and nights asking each other 'Please teach me, how can I love you?' When you are cold and lonely, when you go far away inside, when you forget to ask me 'How can I love you?' I will be here asking you, 'Please help me. How can I love you? We must spend eternity asking this of each other and there is not a day to lose."

December 19

"I have turned the soil here for centuries. My heart has not missed an inch."

December 20

"You never know when our time each day will begin or if you and I will be together at all. You get busy, then sad with your forgetfulness. I see you through all my faces. Then sooner or later our time comes directly. I move in closer. I love your anticipation, your vulnerability, your unworthiness, your fear we may never be total lovers again. The moments we are apart, there are no guarantees. Then the instant it is you and I again, all of life is a guarantee. This is how it must be."

December 21

"I trap you in your own thoughts and feelings. I enclose upon you until you can do nothing without me. You cannot sleep until you ask 'Are we ready?' Before you invite me into your dreams, I must say a few more words. Then as you begin drifting off I am already there before you. When we are this close, you lie down inside of me. We reach one another in the same pause of surrender. Your body is mine to love. I am your joy. And in my womb is the final peace.

"My words today are fallen angels. Each word coming just for you could come from no greater place. Today peace is in the most simple things. Peace begins here and ends here, in each simple step, the smallest gesture, the glance, the brief smile, each second expands and expands into peace."

FIRST SUNSET IN ASSISI

"At the edge of the light, as you risk to enter, you will see all of the Father, all of the Mother, every brother, every sister you have known through time. In this great light, just at the edge of your world, all love welcomes you home. Nowhere else on this earth is the door so open to you. As you enter all memories of home flood you as all who are dear welcome you home. Come join all the family that greets you!"

FINALLY BEFORE GOING TO SLEEP

"You know how good it feels to be home in your own room, your own bed after a long time away. Imagine how good I feel to have you here where I can really take care of you. You know how good it feels to be home where each meal is prepared to your liking and all the little joys are just exactly as you wish them. Imagine how good I feel to have you home again so I can love you exactly as I really want to. Holidays, family reunion—we are all of this and so much more.

"After a day or two of just relaxing, you will share with me everything, then gradually admit all the difficulties being so far away from home. Meanwhile all of love's servants, my saints and angels will be touching you and reminding you where everything is."

December 22

"Home. After the initial excitement of your return, the seeing of old friends and places so dear, you have to ask yourself 'Why did I leave in the first place? Where did the separation begin? How does a child not feel the love of a perfect mother and father? How would a lover turn away from such an all-giving partner? What inside made me leave such a home which has been left waiting in my absence?'

"I, too, ask these questions. Most of all I ask what I now can do to convince you of your complete freedom to stay? How can I make clear that the past is over? Now you belong here with me! We are ready to live together again. Ours is a totally possessive love completely free of definition. Neither of us can be wholly ourselves without the other. Only in this overwhelming dependency can we rise for the great surrender. You must stay home if we are to be everything together!"

December 23

VISITING SAN DAMIANO, ASSISI

"Didn't I promise you snow at San Damiano? Didn't I promise you a winter rose? At the beginning of your walk and again in the garden, snow falls one, two, three flakes at a time, just enough for love's presence to announce itself. All this of course under a clear sky. I love watching you feel my love. Then just when you think it is all over, the snow starts again, three, four, five flakes, then more. These flakes are the angels' delight. The winter rose is mine. The garden is ours to stay in forever. What more needs to be said? Each day I will announce more of the peace which is coming.

"Tonight you see the star guiding me. It's calling you, all of you. You have to be so small to feel how large it is. This star is all of my love, all of my peace, which is destined for the world. This star enlightens my soul, lights my altar, preparing me to give birth to the final peace of peace. Join me. Join me on the entire journey. I am human with all feelings. Love includes all feelings. Join me and help me feel it all. Then curl up and feel what I carry in my womb. Lie in me, right beside Him. Let me carry you both. Let me give birth to you. May my peace in you come out side by side with my greatest love."

December 24

I AWAKEN TO FIND ONE VERY LARGE STAR LIGHTING THE CLEAR BLUE SKY

"You enter the silence alone in me. Today even joy can be a distraction from my humility. To join me is to join the hope of peace that collects your soul, cracked into a thousand pieces. You know only I can put you all together. This is the meaning of peace. Absolute dependence, absolute love and my gift, your birth into peace."

CHRISTMAS EVE AT THE GATE TO CLARE'S GARDEN IN SAN DAMIANO

"You pray, holding love's hand at the gate to all of my joy."

December 25

I AWAKEN TO THE FIRST SNOW IN ASSISI ON CHRISTMAS DAY IN FORTY YEARS

"Didn't I promise you I would announce more peace every day? What better way, what better day to show my greatest love than a foot of snow in Assisi on Christmas? And always your greatest and truly only problem is that you cannot take my love literally enough."

December 26

"Your journey ends but not without seeing one of the most beautiful mosaic ceilings in the world. Here I am being crowned in Heaven. And if I rule, imagine all at my means to love you."

December 27

"You are returning home but home is only in relation to me. Home is the quality of our love, our moments we take with one another. Life without this quality, without these moments, offers no home at all. The only real security is your acceptance of my never-ending humble invitation. Tenderness and intimacy must rule our home together. And so much of the burden of this love rests upon you. No matter how much I am here, you must take my softness, you must feel my joy or it's as if I am not here at all. I am the all-powerful love which rests fully only in a beggar's arms. It's in the beggar's arms that my sweetness can give and give and give until you receive the power and dignity that love deserves."

December 28

"Separations of any kind are voices out of distance from my ears. Speak to me and see how quickly what is lost is reunited. Separations are always a sign of some form of independence trying to survive without love. What is distance but an attempt to live without me, a thought determined to survive without love."

December 29

"You desire to feel me in all the ways I can be for you. Then every moment of every day be a simple bowl of water for all my little flowers."

December 30

"Your memories are current moments for me. Love is never something of the past but happening now over and over again. Your memories are a secret well of our bottomless joy. Here we can draw upon and re-experience each nuance, each subtle feeling of what we have together. No need to look ahead for more when we are already so much. Now is the time to feel what we have been knowing—this is just the beginning to what we are always to be."

December 31

"The year ends as the next must begin. New commitments, more promises, never enough awe for the desperate love, the human paradise which is ours. New Year's resolutions? Every experience, every feeling, each day held sacred. Not a moment alone, not a moment too short to exclude me and through me all the earth and the Heavens. In the delicate wonder may we be overjoyed."

January 1, 1987

"A new season . . . Let me carve you out from the inside into a large beautiful bowl. Let me take your life. I will mold the perfect harmony. I will remove some relationships for your and their new purpose. I will smooth others as they move right next to your soul for all of your enjoyment. What is there to be afraid of? Even if I emptied your life entirely, what do you need when you have me? Even if my love's truth cut to the bone and through it, imagine how close I would be, right next to your bare soul.

"Trust me. Only my love can form you and shape you into the perfect bowl for you and all the others coming to be renewed. Trust me. I must make room for our perfect happiness together. I know your weaknesses. I know just how much support you need and where. What does our love mean if you do not allow me to serve you fully? Trust me. Who better than I to carve your life into a proud and humble masterpiece?"

"Ours is no longer a contest of how true or how much is our love. Ours is no longer a test of wills, yours or mine or how much of each. You have resigned to me. I am always surrendered to you.

"Now love's mystery possesses you, my Holy Grail. Your entire life is the desire for its possession. You are full of such hope and such hopelessness as I spread my love out in front of you. Every day I hear you cry inside as you feel again our love's immense landscape. I must reach into all the faraway places, the silent small hearts inside of you that nobody sees or knows but me. I must be gently with you everywhere love has been forgotten or forbidden. We must settle inside where we have never known each other before. You must be always willing to give me more of yourself, your self-interests.

"Today you say you want to turn everything over to me. And I say I want even more until you are nothing but mine."

"I must be all the little cornerstones in your life as well as your one great love. No more relationships with little compromises, of seeming convenience, or with unspoken truth. Next to me everyone in your life is just right or inappropriate, nothing in between. Each moment with each person is either true or it is not. Next to me, you see all the blemishes and all the treasure in each soul. The only question is whether this person joins you now on the journey for the great peace or his life moves another way. The time is for you to let go and breathe with mountains of fresh honesty. Let everyone come and go as true for them as we walk down the aisle into the silent glory, the altar which has no applause.

"Why should you have anything in your life which does not fit when we fit so well? Better to wear me more closely to you and let others be themselves. What you are each day must be who you are inside perfectly. You can no longer

invest hope where there is no hope when I am everything. And I am yours."

January 4

"This morning in the middle of a large winter storm, I awaken you with the cheer of spring. In winter I pick you up. I must touch my love with spring-fresh flowers, new smells, lots of colors, sunshine and love's beginnings again and again. To know me is to feel the thirst for spring every day. To desire me is to want all the life of spring. To receive my love is to feel me pouring spring all over you and into you until only wildflowers cover you and grow out of your hands and your feet."

January 5

"Today blue sky and sunshine but we continue where we left off yesterday. There is no weather, no obstacle that comes between us. Our love melts the cold. Our love bridges all distance. Our love pierces every difficulty with innocence. Our love grows in every challenge, blooms in every season, and cries out 'Yes, yes, yes' into every sky—day and night.

"Our love is like the many small birds beneath your tree. Every morning they are always hungry, always excited."

January 6

"Why would a love that is so true be so difficult? There can only be one reason and this is because our love is so great. We are much more than a thought or understanding. This love is more than knowing my existence and living more relaxed because I am real and with you.

"Each prayer, feeling, each act of surrender fuels the flames. Every day you must become more conscious as the fire consumes more of you. The coals burn slowly and deeply where you are still asleep, frightened or ashamed.

Each leap of joy comes with a demand as the flame pulls you more into the fire itself. And each moment you live in my center you become part of my creation, creating life with me. As two small cells in an act of love can meet and create a human being, one small flame of ours can build to a fire which will resurrect the world."

January 7

"I am here to lift you, your body, your life, your all. I am here to lift you. There is a high and holy place where only love belongs. This place cannot be for part of you, leaving anything behind. You must place your entire soul into me. My hands become your chest and I hold you as a beautiful, small bird with a red heart, singing. I release you and you go as high as you will fly. My hands wait to hold you again upon your return. Lift yourself and with you all of the earth. Be lifted, rest, then be carried anew. I am here, cheering, listening to your heart beat and sing, rise and rise again."

January 8

"There is never a question of what or how much to do. There is never a question of what to offer and to whom. There is only giving. Each person at your door, every phone call, every meeting is me asking to be received. You give and give and give to the world by receiving me over and over again. It is always me coming closer. And I come in the disguise of your friends and the strangers coming to meet you. I am the all-joyful, the lonely, the confused in a hundred different circumstances coming, hoping you will always have a moment for me. I am your lover! I am your mother, your father, your child, your brother wanting the only gift which is uniquely yours to offer. I want your love. And the greatest love there is, is to receive me.

"Pray for me, ask for me, beg and scream inside if necessary for me. Reach and keep on reaching into every encounter until you feel me surrounding you constantly, bringing you the fresh flowers of life at every turn."

"Everything is still. I bring you near me and hold you as a beautiful, earthen bowl. I place flower tops along the bottom and all the sides, red, blue, purple, yellow. Between your soul and the world is my love. Everyone comes to you through me. My flowers sweeten your experience of the world and the world's knowledge of you. I am the bouquet of love that stands between you and life. Every moment touches me first, then I give it gently to you. I am at the bottom of the bowl, the closest to you, and all of life is invited. But in truth, you and I are already so much!"

"The loneliness, the separateness, the human feelings day after day pull you to your knees again and again in quest for me. And each time you fall you come deeper inside of me. I give the joy and the pain with only one wish . . . merge with me. Merge with me until you can only breathe my breath, my simple wish, until you are filling my lungs, having forgotten your own.

"The clearest path to love is not on your own two feet but on your knees. But since your two feet call out their way again and again, I can only invite you to my humble place and take your hands between mine as we pray together inseparably."

"Humility is the tallest mountain. Humility is the unbreakable stone. Anything else is not humility but weakness in disguise. As simplicity is not to be confused with limitation, humility is nothing less than absolute truth, absolute strength. The day will come when you will know my absolute love and you will disappear into my most beautiful unknown. When you take this awesome knowledge, all strength is yours and there are only simple, humble steps, one after another forever after.

"Our love can be defeated by any army. Our love is at the mercy of each thought, each feeling. Our love can be run over, denied, abandoned in ten thousand ways. And it is exactly because it is so defenseless that it grows and grows and grows. What I feel for you, what I am, is without opposition. Our love, the words stand in their own mist, naked yet hidden from everything but you and me. You join me and I exist. You join me and you exist as if for the first time."

January 12

"The march begins. Every giant step within to me, a new fresh step into the world. Every new opening, a place for me to fulfill. We make each new step together, then you feel all the world in your hands and the green grass at your feet. We take another step and you hold up the world anew. Together we are part of the great march where each individual is deciding to pick up the world knowing its very survival depends on everyone. Each soul now must bow down for hundreds and stand up for all humanity. Without me there is no step at all. With me, all of love is at your feet, your heart, your forehead, welcoming you. Heaven is being collected in the most primitive villages, the most private hearts soon to be released in all the winds."

January 13

"You come in and I take off your shoes. All you have to do is sit and simply feel. Let me fill the room. Let me occupy your senses. Simply watch me and listen. Record these small moments over and over again until you sense my movements around you every day, always. Feel me making you more and more comfortable. I love to sing as I serve you. I know exactly how your day has been and all I need is your presence, your openness, for me to take each care into hand. Tonight I wash your feet before you begin another journey. I must do this slowly. You allowing me to touch you like this humbles me beyond your knowing. This physical caring is the servant's secret about love, my purest joy."

January 14

"Over and over again you pray 'Make me more sensitive to you. Help me to love you. Teach me how to listen and feel. How can I stay close to you? Help me!' These are the words that feed love. Without them love withers and dies for the winter. Together with your gentle requests, my hopeful answers, spring comes again and again in all seasons. Love climbs and climbs out of the earth into our Heaven.

"Do not be afraid of the shroud of love, the cover of winter. Fall hopelessly inside and let me hold you and hold you until spring begins again."

January 15

ON THE FERRYBOAT WITH TEARS IN MY EYES AT THE
BEAUTY OF THE SAN JUAN ISLANDS

"The motion of the boat, the light in the air, each new horizon, all of this is not my waters, not my islands and mountain peaks but ours. Here my ear is right next to your heart. My heart is right next to your lips . . . I don't want to miss a single cry of desire . . . satisfied.

"The day will come when you will put your arms around me, hold me, and never let go. We will dance and dance. I will unfold in your arms, revealing myself in a thousand wonderful ways and new feelings. You will melt again and again. In truth we will not know whose arms are around whom, who is holding the other up and who is leading."

January 16

THE SAN JUAN ISLANDS, SNOW-CAPPED MOUNTAINS, SMALL INLETS, PRIVATE BAYS

"The peace, the endless peace . . . There is so much to feel. And you are afraid to feel because you do not know if the feelings would ever stop. You are afraid you will become lost. You will lose your identity and all of your limiting purpose. My peace will bury who you think you are. You know you have nothing, you are nothing more or less than one soul in my glorious landscape.

"Now and when you spoke to the large group the other night, you could not find any self-importance because you know where you stand in my infinite terrain: one single soul who has opened his eyes and heart enough to feel my wind touch down in his lungs before moving on. In the vastness, the endless quiet, I invite you to become lost if necessary, if this is how you will settle into my simple purpose for you. I invite you to feel who you are without meaning, if necessary, if this is how you will finally let me simply give to you. I am boundless and yet isn't my love more personal every day? Am I not more present in each sunset, each wave retreating from the shore?"

January 17

DURING THE RETREAT

"I place my words on your tongue for you to taste. I put my hand on your heart for you to remember. I do this for

36

you and it is up to you whether to share me and all the joy. I need you for you and not as someone to give my love away. You expose all of your desire. Shamelessly you humble me in front of everyone and I have no choice but to pour my love upon you."

January 18

THE RETREAT CONTINUES

"I know your dilemma. You stand in front of the people without anything to give. You can only admit your desire. I stand a few feet away in waiting, watching you dangle in your dependency. Then I swoop in and pick everyone up. As you see me in each soul about you, I swoop in over and over again as an excited swallow over his nest."

January 19

"You are staying with friends who want a baby. You meet other good friends who thirst for a child. You sleep and work in children's rooms. Feelings of babies and children are everywhere. I could not ask you more directly to come closer, to be my son. My son! How sweet the word. My little boy. You cannot be too small, too dependent for me. It is only the son who feels all of his mother's and father's love who can bring souls finally home to stay.

"Imagine all the love I have for my son, all the little joys I have watching out for his wishes. Can it be surprising that I enjoy satisfying his desires even before he is aware of them?"

January 20

"Time is accelerating and collapsing. What was going to be left for tomorrow is happening today. Pray, hold the new order. Pray placing your soul in the heart of the new universe. Everyone is now given the opportunity. Each soul is descending or ascending to the far reaches of love. The result is the same. You know the depths of each height. You know the heights capable with each fall into humble acceptance. Your fingers stretch outward and outward around the globe until your hands meet again, coming together in prayer, gently touching your lips. All hope joins you. Each prayer is another spark of brilliant light for the new paradise."

January 21

"You are God's son. He is the only one to hold onto. There is no substitute. Not the saints, even I, love itself cannot be worshipped. There is only God. He is the only source for all of your needs. He is the only provider. God, only God is your home, your friend, your daily comfort.

"My poor child, hearing these words is for you like getting undressed when you thought you were already without clothes, without anything but yourself. Receiving God is to be more naked than yourself. He is found underneath, after all your selfish interests, after all of yourself. This nakedness, this vulnerability is your only repose."

January 22

"You are so happy when you see all the small birds feeding in your winter garden. When they eat what you offer them, you feel filled with purpose. Now you know how I feel when you come to me and take out of my hand. There is no greater happiness than to feed you and all of my small ones. I wait till I see you coming. When you draw near, I am all expectant, ready to offer you the very best of what I have to give. And when you look into my heart and feel what I want for you, you and I are both overflowing."

January 23

"The path to holiness is unworthiness. There is no other. You cannot tie your shortcomings in a knot and try to hide them. You cannot pretend they are not there or do not matter. The purer you become, the larger they grow in front of you. You can only confess, admitting once and for all how undeserving you are to inherit so much love. And after you make your admission, the next day when you are filled with doubts or find yourself lonely to the point you hurt from isolating me once more from your life, you must confess again. Offer me everything which tries to occupy my place.

"The path of unworthiness tells you love is yours not because you are special, having attained some discipline over your most human feelings. Love is your inheritance. It is given no matter how guilty or fearful you may be. This inheritance is given equally to all. It's up to you to admit your unworthiness often, if you want to enjoy all the tenderness and awe which is meant for you. I cannot help but send my angels bearing gifts to the soul that opens to me and says 'But I am so unworthy.'

"You have so much to receive, beginning with my endless love and your immortality, not to mention your destiny with me as your wife, your husband, your mother, your father, your all. How could you not feel unworthy? Since I understand so well, why not simply offer it to me, moment by moment."

January 24

"Remember in your unworthiness to ask for everything beautiful. The problem is never your unworthiness to ask but the vestiges of pride that still keep you separate from me. A child naturally asks for everything he wants and expects every request to come true. And why not?

"In your unworthiness be like one of the great tall ships, filled with my treasure. Let me be your cargo, fill your sails, and stand never more than a step away as the perfect shipmate, ready for every order. Even before you give the word, I am providing for you. So never cease telling me what you want. Give the command so my love can become more exact, more precise, closer and closer to just the spot that humbles itself, so open, so very ready, so expectant for me."

January 25

"You heard me speak in your community tonight when the woman said 'Safety is bare bones.' This is true. There is nothing to wear, no thoughts which will protect you. There is nowhere to hide, no feelings which will shield you. Safety is bare bones. And in truth you would want it no other way. I am always just beneath the skin, the surface of things. I am always in the bottom of the most open space, the most tender place. If you are willing to look, this is where I am. If there is no hurt for me to rest in, I am next to each bone, the core of each relationship. My love is what binds you, binds one another. And where I am is the only safety. My love strips you to the ground. I reduce you to bare bones. And have you ever known such richness and sweetness? Have you ever lived with less fear?

"On my knees, with tears of pure love, I ask you, 'Please let me take you down even further. Let me take you until you are wholly mine.'"

January 26

"You have a sore throat. Your body feels weak and sore. Remember last night when you found yourself talking and something deeper inside said, 'Be empty, only listen.'? Make your suffering a positive joy. Spend this time making apologies to all whom you entertain with your words instead of my heart. There is only one purpose for any discomfort and this is to bring you closer to me. The greater the pain, the greater the opportunity of our meeting.

"Suffering is something that is never yours alone but ours. It is not something to defeat because you would also be defeating your need for me. It is not something to dull or ignore because it is love itself begging to be felt. Suffering is always me with my packages, my presents and my need for your help to stretch and reach more to me. Together we must open this pain as a bow of string tied around greater depths of love.

"Suffering is not something to hold onto and take glory in. There is no glory besides me. A moment of pain, no matter how long, is just long enough to show you the way to my humble door. Pain great or small is always just as necessary as our admission that we need one another. There would never be another moment of discomfort in the entire world if we all lived knowing how much we need the love of the other. Today's pain as always is your separation from me. Feel every small corner of discomfort and invite me into this place. You will find I am already there waiting for you."

January 27

"When you judge others very rarely, the few judgements you do have can make a terrible mark. Better you judged others all the time and you and they would not take them so seriously.

"The moment you are about to label someone and announce their faults, you are really admitting your own helplessness to see love in them right now. So the only answer is to make no announcement at all and give me your helplessness. Your never-ending question to me must be, 'Can you help me to see love in this moment?' And when you fail instead of blaming others, ask me again. By yourself, you are incapable of determining. Remember the pressure you feel, the tension, the constant creeping in of separateness is not yours but mine. Certainly I would not ask for your total dependence upon me unless I also told you every difficulty is mine as well. Don't fight my battles. Simply be my constant friend, my remembered one, and help me to not forsake a single soul through our compassion."

January 28

"The places of self-doubt are where you hold yourself instead of me. Each small spot where I am excluded may as well be your entire life because one doubting thought has the power to brush across the entire canvas of our love. But only for a moment. I come back again and again with new strokes filled with new colors of gentleness and hope. Each time I try to paint over exactly this place where you yet believe you are alone and without me. Every day this is my will to get to this small dark point which by contrast seems to deny all of me and what we have. Our love cannot invade the darkness. We cannot take it over or rub it out. Love can only wish for each thought of self to give up to something greater. Our love can only trust and trust until every thought of doubt can find no other choice but to join us."

January 29

"First thing every morning we give to each other while starting the day. Right away you begin offering me your thoughts, your plans, your little wishes to be close. Haven't we agreed your entire effort is for our constant reunion? You have aimed yourself the best you can in my direction. What more could I ask for?

"Since I am the target, do you think you could miss? Do you think I would trick you or make your task more difficult for any reason? Is there any way I would refuse you your goal by keeping myself distant or unapproachable? You know all you need is to hold your desire before me and I cannot help but make every circumstance, every encounter one more incident of me demonstrating my love. Your desire is enough to humble me day after day until all I can do is be here for you and give you my innermost peace. With such desire, I cannot help but be in the foreground and the background, all around you. You and I can be nothing less."

January 30

"You desire greater poverty to be certain you live only for my love. I desire only greater riches for you to be certain of how much love I have for you.

"In truth, when you live for me, life will always be rich. When you live for yourself, no matter how many things you have around you, you will be destitute, poorer than the poor. The crown of glory rests upon the head of poverty. The golden slippers wait for the feet that have felt the tenderness of the earth's soil. And love, only love and more love is for those who give themselves away for the comfort of another."

January 31

"What others hope to find in new lovers, work, or a nice home, you find it all in me. While they worry over and wait for their desires, you let me feed you directly every day. I am always in front of you simply. Why search and struggle for love some place far away or with someone who feels so little? Why ever settle for less again when I am more and more? Our only limit is your appetite for my finest strokes, my lightest touches. While others struggle for control over their lives, you surrender your helplessness right away. The world is the looking glass through which we discover one another, never something to possess for itself. We are committed to being fully alive, here and in the world beyond. We must be always ready to ride my joy and fly."

February 1

"Accept refuge in me, in the emerald palace. When you are in pain, joy, indecision, when you simply want to be more yourself, take refuge in me. No matter how you feel forced into a corner, there is always enough space to take refuge in me. And when you are in an open field with all the wild flowers dancing at your feet, take refuge in me and the field will be even greater.

"I am the way in and the way out. Just start with the most recent memory of love and I am already here. Then begin asking me to take you more into love itself. As you join me, you must be willing to let go of everything which is not love. But I am here to help you. Give me everything which seemingly does not belong with us and I will find its place. I am your great refuge. You are not escaping but taking your small life into the great life which is ours. The day will come when you will realize you are a refuge for me, the palace that love can always come to. In these times there are so few hearts that consistently have a place for me."

February 2

"Loneliness is the result of the struggle for earthly rewards. The aloneness is always the fear of the helplessness to fall into greater arms than your own, to be held in the infinite compassion. The madness of your independence is nothing, simple fear of love. As the soil hugs the roots of every flower and tree, the whole earth yearns to hold each soul and support you in your true purpose. Purpose cannot help but fill you upon acceptance of your pure dependence. Walk in the earth and no longer over her. Let the sky come down upon you. Take my love personally. All of the earth and Heaven is incomplete until it touches you. Join the many birds in your garden taking shelter from the rain under the leaves of my flowers. Each leaf stands tender guard while they feed upon the seeds on the ground."

February 3

"Only love knows if a soul is served the most being bathed in love's glory or completely emptied until the soul's walls crack from need. Love's glory can become taken for granted and lose its holiness. Emptiness can become a compromise with pain instead of a sacred desert ready to bloom. The heart of the saint is an ordinary bucket filled to feed the thirsty, then emptied in order to know whom one feeds. The bucket is filled again with the divine only to become bone dry sometime later.

"You find faith in the ecstasy and die in the emptiness. Someday you may join the saints who die in the ecstasy and find faith in the hollow cells of their aloneness. The bliss and agony are equal gifts, love's rewards. Once embraced, love makes new promises in all of the moments of greatest tenderness. Love sits at the bottom of the darkest spot. Love must touch the feeling that is most alone and separate from all the others. Then love's intensity grows some more with ever greater innocence."

February 4

"Pray not to my ears because I hear you even before you open your lips. Pray to my heart so I may surround you and take you into me. It is the infusion of your soul into me that slowly covers you in my simplicity and acceptance. Offer your soul for my hands to lift to my chest and take deeply within. Only this union will settle all the unrest. Prayer is the only resolution to the struggles, the running streams of worry and doubt that have nowhere to go. Prayer takes all of you into the great hall to merge with something greater.

"Prayer guarantees that no part of you will escape the peace, the quiet body which is ours. The circumstances in everyone's life sooner or later reach a point where only prayer is left. Sooner or later love is recognized as the only solution for every soul. Prayer is love's sure invitation. Upon simple prayer love enters all situations. Prayer is always the entrance way humble enough for love to march through in holy triumph."

"There are many fruits of this love of ours. There is the security, the peace, the many blessings. But perhaps the one most overlooked is the clear path that is made to the deepest cry within you. With me in your life, you can feel how much you really want love. The closer we are, the more we become, the more present this desire is. Nothing else will do. From the abyss inside of you comes the scream for love. All the while you are falling into my ever-deeper embrace. Let's pray you never lose track of this cry because perhaps more than anything else, your need is the guarantee that I am always with you. And if you stay just on the edge of this cry you cannot help but feel me right next to you, wiping each tear with my joy."

"You think your self-worth is in what you do. But what happens after you are a parent, when all the people go home from your retreats, when the birds fly away full from the food you leave them? What is your self-worth when it is just you and me? And why do you need to find something to make my love acceptable? What could make you worthy of all that I am for you?

"As long as you are looking for reasons for our love, my grace becomes a little less. As long as you try to substantiate what we are together, you make us smaller. As long as you insist on trying to find something within you to prove that you are worthy of all of this, you are occupying time and space where more love could be present.

"What we are could never have anything to do with what you do, what you have to offer, or any other measurement of how good or better you may become. There is nothing you really can do to earn more or push me away. I am always here as soon as you stop these fearful efforts. Humility is such a painful sword but you must use it on every part of yourself until it feels there is nothing left. It is when you stop that I can begin truly loving you.

"The only genuine gift you have for me is to be present. Be available for me to talk to and touch. Be here for me, so I can feel I truly have someone to love. Give me all the little parts of yourself, no thought or feeling is too small. Give me your all including your excuses not to give me more. When you are like this, worthiness and all your other cares do not exist. How could they? It's only you and me . . ."

February 7

"For the little deaths you endure, I build a beautiful tomb with white columns covered with green vines and purple blossoms, a tomb full of sweet life. These small ego deaths guarantee our life together forever. Today's sacrifices are today's rewards, as instantly our love spreads into new dimensions. One less cornerstone of self, the more steps for us and our relationship without boundaries. Everything human is called until nothing human is resisted. Every discomfort is asked for until there is no discomfort, for nothing is kept separate from me. Every pain is a new anchor where I am more deeply lodged in the soul, incapable of sailing into love's wonder without you again."

February 8

"Your prayers to support others in the midst of their terrible winter is answered with the experience of your own winter. As you call me to embrace the darkness, you and they feel relief. Only my love gives meaning where there is none. Only my light fills the empty night of the soul with purpose. You give less than nothing when you join others in their hopeless moments without me. You give all there is when you share your eager dependence upon your loved one, calling upon me again and again. Pray that the whole world learns to call me as such, quickly and frequently, for love's large and small favors."

February 9

"Death of the soul does not exist. Only the body and mind can die. Open the pure curtain between us and you will see life forever. All of love is so close to you. Accept the pure veil between us and you feel and hear that which before you only imagined. The body is born and dies for this purpose. The mind has no other true end except for you to accept your own purity and that in others. With such acceptance death does not exist. The curtain is drawn and nothing is withheld. All of love, including loved ones throughout time, stand by in anticipation of the reunion."

February 10

"Someday you will look back and see the physical trials of life as just the windy path, the dirt for us to walk upon. Every hardness, the sharp attacks of loneliness, the breaking, the crumbling of everything around the soul is all part of the great falling down of the human walls. Everything between you and me, between you and you, is crushed into small stones, then eventually crushed even further into fresh earth. Physical life is just this, the trail of the spirit, the daily course you set to serve me, bringing us ever closer. Each stretch you bring not only yourself but everyone with you. Next to the stones, haven't there always been flowers along the way? Learn to welcome every twist and turn, the steep and gentle slopes. Give your mind and body wholly to every detail until nothing is left but you and me, one love."

February 11

"Amends, amends, amends for laziness, forgetfulness, the ever-present head of doubt and sinking heart of hope.

Make amends, this is what the Father, the Mother, the bride and groom, all the hosts of love want. When someone takes the time and asks for your forgiveness and continued love—doesn't his request melt your heart? So you can imagine how I feel every time you return to me and our quest. Remember through each soul the whole earth is lifted or put down. No feeling, no experience is too small to make amends for, then be carried to its Heavenly place. Be my amended heart and I will be your constant savior."

February 12

WHEN THINKING ABOUT MY LONELINESS

"Who better than I to lead your soul to the waters that will refresh you? Who better than I to match your soul in Heaven and lead you to a partner to love you? Who better than I to plan the little details for love's joy, arrange the circumstances for love's surprise, and prepare the days ahead for your continual happiness?

"It is my truest wish for you to experience my love fully. So how could I withhold anything from you? Love does not include suffering. If you suffer it's only in the preparation to receive my love. Your wedding bed has been made. Now let me fulfill your desires and free your soul for more and more love."

February 13

"I rub your soul like fine sandpaper. Of course, sometimes my most gentle touch is for you like an avalanche of snow crashing upon the rocks below. I continue rubbing. Ours is an agreement made a long time ago.

"You feel me carving you, leading you into the unknown. You are the hard wood and I am the simple artist. If I were to tell you that I too am the wood, I too live in the unknown, would this frighten you? Love knows not what it leads to. I simply trust myself in you, in everyone, to take the next step when love is ready.

"In truth we rub each other like fine sandpaper. I hesitate. I too am shy, never certain how much you will be with me. When you stop and suddenly take me inside further then ever before, I cannot help but feel your love as an avalanche taking me into new depths. I risk to go with each soul into this shared journey, so beautiful and out of anyone's control. Love takes us only as far as we are willing. Something in each moment is the only assurance to continue. This love is in you and between us, the interaction that no soul alone can know without another, without me.

"I am the great peace rubbing against you willing to hear everything you hear. I hear all the interference with you. If you are willing I feel everything you feel. So who is the great artist? Who is leading whom? I just want you to hold me, hold me, hold me, then please hold me some more."

February 14

"Your weaknesses and triumphs become something when you give them to me. Alone you are so small and with me, the smallest self becomes the speck of God's holiness greater than any marble monument. For life's meaning give yourself away over and over again to me. For love, practice noticing how much I feel and receive you every time you come."

February 15

"Every day I am here for you. During this time you cannot run away, pretend, or in any way make me less than what I am. Now we have moments each day, face to face. When are you going to hold me longer? I pray for the time when my gentleness is not such a confrontation but simply my gentle touch, touching you. My fingers touch your cheeks. My hand lifts your chin. Our eyes meet. What is there to be afraid of? What could I possibly do to prove once and for always what my love is and how much it is yours? All

I can do is invite your eyes to meet me again and again until you do not look away and there is no more need for invitations."

February 16

" A s you prepare for another journey, the flowers in your front yard are all in bloom. The whole garden opens and waves goodbye waiting for your return. A new life, a new love will be returning with you. Love knows when new love is being born. Every other part of you will just have to wait and be surprised."

February 17

ON THE LONG PLANE RIDE TO ZURICH

" T ime exists in the moments you are separate from me. Otherwise there is only me and you. All other experience is time wasting until our reunion. Our love implants the sweetness of eternity into each instant. There is not an occasion that is not transformed when I am included. There is not an occasion that does not hold a unique opportunity for us to be alive and in each other's heart as never before.

"Do you know how many rooms are in each chamber of my heart? I could spend a lifetime leading you through the many palaces and orchards inside that exist only for love. And we still would not have begun to explore the grand suites and sitting rooms inside the castles overlooking mountaintops which sit empty, waiting just for you.

"From now on, time is nothing more or less than me calling you. It is me beckoning you to join me in yet another room with another view of eternity, which is no longer something faraway but right here, exploding in peace and sweetness. Ours is yet another place inside that you will never know until our love becomes what it is. And while we sit and enjoy the views, what better thing to do than invite all your family and friends to sit with us too?"

February 18

WHILE RECOVERING FROM LACK OF SLEEP

"Be like me with no body. See how many souls I can receive. And if your body persists in wanting to be noticed, let it be as empty as possible so there is lots of room for every soul you meet and of course always more and more space for me.

"With your body as just a meeting place, does it really matter exactly what shape it is in? What's important is our meeting. So don't let me lose a moment of your attention."

February 19

"You are still full of self, even if it's your empty self. You take up so much of the bowl with your words, your past, that I have less room than I want to fill you, fulfill you.

"You are lonely because there is still mostly room just for yourself inside. When the day comes and you are truly empty for me and your friends to fill you, to be within you, you will not have thoughts of loneliness again.

"Loneliness is always too much self with not enough room for others. Be empty like the frozen ponds under the snow. Be unseen, water under the ice. Be liquid, ready for anyone to join you, resisting nothing, expectant always of my company."

<hr>

February 20

"Believe in me, nothing else. The details of your life are the details of my love waiting for your belief. Believe in me, only me. It is always me reaching out and if you don't find me, certainly do not turn away. Stay open. I am here, never far.

"Believe in me, for your all. You can never search deep enough, not that I am not easily available. But it's in the depths of your search that I can truly open to all of you.

"Believe in me, so I can pull you under, no longer tempted by any earthly rewards. Wrapped in my blanket of love, I carry you underneath, down the earthly mountains to the mountaintops of Heaven. Look at all that is before us . . .

"If you want to serve more and more, you must be less and less. If you want to give more and more, you must be more and more empty with nothing but me to offer.

"And if you want to love, you must hold out your wish for love. You must admit your greatest hunger, if you wish to feed others . . . And if you really want to touch others, you must let me touch you like I have never before . . ."

<hr>

February 21

"Words can distract from the feeling, no matter how much you try. Better to leave love in the silence where you can see more clearly, left only in the clutches of trust.

"I bring love together as near as you will take her. You can no longer hide in the words. Simply because you hear me this is not enough. You must submerge in what I bring you. You must risk drowning in this love and trust you can breathe under my largest wave. You cannot see where I take you and at the same time be where you are. You are being pulled into my undertow, where only the heart can survive. The eyes and ears know nothing. I cannot rescue you and at the same moment pull you as deeply as you wish to go. Simply try not to resist. Let go into your own destiny. There are no guideposts beyond your feelings."

February 22

"Whenever in doubt about the motivation of your life, whether your love is selfish or the kind of love that will grow into more emptiness for others to join you inside . . . call upon the great love to help you. Call upon the Holy Mother, the Holy Father, the true hosts of love to show you the difference between love to fulfill a need and love to surpass all needs. Ask the great love to take you beyond the temptation to find relief. Love is not for overlooking more difficult feelings but to find true peace, where all feelings come home in the silence. Call upon the greatest love to come down to the smallest question of all, so all answers will be only me.

"Call upon the greatest love to carry you into the far reaches of love somewhere in the silent here and now. If you allow me to carry you far enough, beyond the noise of your resistance, my love will guide you into the silence that is no longer lonely or empty but filled with the love that is holy."

February 23

"May we be nothing more and nothing less than what you want for us to be. What perfection to give to another how they want to be given to. What an opportunity to love not how you would try to imagine or control love but love with love itself as the complete orchestration.

"The only task is the willingness to hear. To let each note sing in the body as it gently reverberates from one chamber of yours to mine. Love is the symphony passed back and forth between hearts, each note being personally carried with the growing joy of sharing the true sound. And the true sound is my love for you. The joy in knowing you are here listening. Our sound goes where there is no sound.

Love is what fills the ocean between souls where nothing else can. Love is the only music that the great silence will allow to enter because it is selfless, as giving as emptiness itself. Love in the silence has nowhere else to go but to fill your eyes with tears spreading throughout the universe with knowledge of itself, of love. As love pours into the space where it is most welcome, love is nothing more than our willingness to be loved. The silence calls. I sing, silently praying to be heard. I love you. Do you know the joy I have when I arrive after my long journey? No sooner do I land than I want to be off with you again. I love you. In each note I am taken. There is only one place meant for me to go and this is toward you, never certain I will be received until I am.

"Sometimes I have to be separate from you before you can really see me. It is when you risk to really let go and let me go that I can come to you as I really am. The shawl around my head is your shawl. You gave it to me. The smile on my face is your smile, all the love I feel from you. And when my arms went around you, of course a dear friend had to stand and embrace you for me. Because we are now a physical love, so close because we are not afraid to say good-bye. Thank you for this. I love you."

February 24

"In every real love there is a little sacrifice. You give me some of the joy. You give me some of the boundless peace. You give me some of the love. And this is what happens in the moments of separation. You have given me all with none for yourself, not knowing when I will give love back. This great act, this gift is what makes love grow. I always return stronger, thanks to your faith. It is in your willingness to give it all away that the small sacrifices become heroic acts of holiness and this is why love is always holy.

"For the saints, love is a continual sacrifice. Their joy, their peace, their love is in giving all the love back to me. The separations are their ecstasy because they know I have welcomed back my gifts and I am now sharing them with others. The love has been sanctified, purified, multiplied by their selfless desire for more and more of others to enjoy this love. And of course, the saints have the most love of all because in their desire to so quickly give it away, I cannot help myself but come more and more, making certain each little detail, each small gesture in their lives is full of love. And this is my greatest wish for you.

"When the day comes that you celebrate the sacrifices, love will have come home to me, bringing you. And together we will never part again."

LATER, BEFORE GOING TO SLEEP

"I just want you to love me. Sometimes you will love me by leaving, so when you return you will have even more to give. Sometimes you will love me with your anger, so when you put down your arms we will have an even greater peace. Sometimes you will love me with your tears over your inability to love me as much as you wish. And always you will love me with your smile saying you feel my love and I love you so much . . .

"You should never miss me because you have me. You have me more than I have myself because I am whole only when possessed by you. So please don't miss me but possess me more and more. There is no greater blessing for me than to be never missed but personally possessed by you in bliss.

"You must practice loving me in others every day. You must see me in all ways. Otherwise I may disappear. I may become less than wonderful. Please give me away so I can be your constant companion. Please never cease giving me away. You are my bride and groom. And I am your everlasting . . ."

February 25

"You have reached the destination inside where you need love all the time. You need the kind attention, to be held and adored. You need someone to be telling you how much they care. You must hear the words 'I love you' over and over or you feel you cannot survive.

"This is how it should be. To know me is not to learn to

survive without love. To know me is to depend upon my love more and more until it is constantly around you. But how could you expect to have such love always around you? Easy. I am here, aren't I? So of course I send my heart of hearts to pick up your every care, hold your every desire, to extend an ever-new invitation for more love.

"And of course this destination you have reached is not the end but simply a new beginning, a plateau before we climb an even greater mountain, reach an even more spectacular height where only perfect love can keep you from falling. And of course you know it is I who will provide all this and more, much more. You have yet to experience how much love your soul needs to be alive. I mean really alive."

--------- *February 26* ---------

"Truth grows the most in the dark where you cannot see or hear. Even your feelings are uncertain. Francis of Assisi spent much time in caves for this very reason. The only love which he was certain was pure was that which grew in the absence of all light. There he knew he was not in love with just a beautiful sight or simply good feelings. He knew he was not in love with just the momentary satisfactions of life. He had to be absolutely certain his love was pure and it was true and only for me. In the dark where his heart could not be fooled, he lay waiting for me.

"There was no confusion about what was my embrace and simple good sensations which could come from the sun or just about anything. Only the most true love would dare to join him in the dark. And when it seized him he knew it was me.

"So while you have so much of love seemingly around you, remember I always enter through the darkness, in the area of doubt and loneliness. Then I come forward to be seen. And late in the night when you are asleep, I cannot help but wake you and say this is me. I want you to know me as I really am. I want you to know me in the dark. Remember all the love filtered through the light and people each day is only a small part of me. We must have these moments in the darkness where I can really be. Come to me here. This is where our love can grow in complete certainty that I am who I say. And it is you that I am seeking.

In the darkness may you never stop seeking me. In the darkness may we meet. You in your emptiness, me in my glory. In the dark may we silently come together . . .

"The darkness comes always at the invitation of resurrection.

"In the darkness your friends are no longer visible. Everyone who says 'I love you' is not there. It is only you and I. In the darkest hour I was left for dead with a thief on either side. Only God knew how alive I really was, how alive I always am. To join me in this hour is the greatest love you can give.

"Give thanks for the dark day. Once again you have found your true love, your true bride. In the absence of light, you have found your pure friend."

February 27

"Your pictures of me can become lost in your mind. Pray I never lose you in my heart. You cannot say this prayer too often. Tell me how bad you feel letting my face and the details of my love disappear into memory. Tell me how you hope your face and your soul don't follow the same fate. What if I forgot you? What if I let you slip by, thinking love is never missed? Never take my loyalty for granted. The promises we make are the only fibers holding us together. You could fall away from me aimlessly if the pull of my love were not so great. Never assume this gravity that has held us fixed in front of one another could not change. Don't let go of my hands in the belief they will always be here waiting for your return.

"I take your heart each moment it is offered to me as if I may never be able to feel you again. The night is vast: all the forces at work great. How can you live assuming my presence unless it follows with your own hard work and commitment? I beg of you, never let my flame go unattended. How can you blindly continue after seeing so much? How can you let your feelings become less than always poised toward me after all we have handed one another? With all the importance I have, how could you let any part of our love be forgotten? What if I became preoccupied? What if I drifted into myself instead of being on constant guard for a soul in trouble?

"Pray I never fall asleep at my watch. Pray I never look another way as you fall into some selfish mood. For love to be real it must be mutual. I cannot be the only one pulling you to keep in touch. Pray your hunger for me is never satisfied. Pray no part of us will ever be assumed replaceable. What we have been, what we are is like the most fragile glass. Don't be distracted. Don't move if there is any chance our love may be dropped. What excuse could ever help if our bond was broken?"

"I shudder to think how precious we are and how much attention this love of ours takes to be guaranteed just for another day, no less eternity. I shudder to think what would happen if I ever offered you anything less than all of me. Please don't lose me in your sights. Please keep me always on the horizon. Let us always be ready to hold the other tight. Let us pray that even the smallest sign of our love will never be misplaced or forsaken."

February 28

"Once love is this close, there is nowhere to hide. No longer can you find refuge in your problems or seeming lack of problems. Your busyness, your illness, your poverty, your aloneness, everything is exposed. Next to me, you can see so clearly how dependent you are, how much love you need, how your life cannot continue without all of my support. Why invest yourself in hiding ever again? I am much too close for this. There is nowhere you can rest except in me. Hide in me and I will protect you from yourself if this is what you need until you are ready to be as naked as I."

"Why do I send someone to represent me in loving you? You have asked for the love that never leaves your side. She has asked to be my truest servant. With you together I can be so much more than with either one of you alone, for love always multiplies with numbers.

"My wishes? Simply surrender to me. You come together to receive me in one another. If I am ever absent, love will be gone. And if I am ever present you will sail into my ocean in my boat with my presence securing every destination. I am in every depth of feeling, preparing you for each approaching wave of tenderness and joy. I bring you together to make a new commitment to serve me in others. As you bathe in me in each other, the joy cannot help but splash out into the world.

"I ask two things: Tell me every day how I can love you. Then have the courage to receive my love even more.

"Now that love is here, you can begin to receive the other side of love. You can begin to take every rejection, every attack, every hardness, every pain that comes your way as a personal message for you to receive me even through this. Every act of fear you witness is meant for you, for it too comes from me. My love now cannot be limited. No matter what form I come in, you must receive it all as if it is I, the purest love, the humblest truth. You can never turn your head again. I am in front of you no matter what you see. And I am always asking to be received."

ON THE WAY TO ASSISI

"These days together are to invite the soul out into the grassy fields, to take my hands and let me lead you into the wildflowers. What is love but an invitation to bring the most precious self out into the open knowing that all of love, the angels, and the earth protect you.

"What is love but an invitation to enter my secret domain where only the lightest light will welcome you. Pass through this love and my breath has passed through your soul. Pass through this love and from now on I will always emerge with you."

March 3

IN ASSISI

"To experience love you must be slower than your fear. Listen to the subtle energies that move you. To experience peace, you must be as slow as peace. Do this now before becoming occupied with something new. No matter how much waits to merge with you, your preparation will determine the outcome. As always I stand with all my joy waiting in my hands. You and the determination of your fear will set my limits."

March 4

IN ASSISI

"The purpose of love: unfold your trust like wings excited then soaring in the great peace. Discover the many places inside holding out against love. Disappear into the soul of another until you both become much larger, no longer certain where one ends and the other begins. The other is now your fingers, your lips, your skin, your eyes looking at you. The other is your great opportunity to love as you have always dreamed of loving me. And it is I waiting for you, happy and at peace."

March 5

"Offer your love to all those who are without love. Offer your joy to all those who hunger for joy. Offer your peace to all those who seek and as yet have not found. Every time you hold hands, offer a hand to someone who has no one to hold. Every time you kiss, offer it to those with no one to kiss them. Offer your love to the angels who have no physical love. Offer your light to the stars who give and give and give. And offer back to God so He and She are embraced."

March 6

"I arrange . . . I arrange. I pull your life together day by day in each moment as I tie the bow around all the loose ends. This is my gift to you. Your gift to me? Your ceaseless efforts to give thanks while continuing to let me arrange your life in the depths of the mystery of my love."

March 7

"Real love reveals the hardened core inside the soul. It's a circle of previous disappointment, events and emotions of all kinds that have become walls of protection around the Heavenly center. Almost all souls live in such an encasement. Only love, the love of my constant attention can truly touch this barrier to real life and love.

"Relationships are my calling to serve one another until the core is identified. Serve one another until the barriers no longer exist. My love is the only protection. While one is giving, the walls of the other are being freed from future fear. As the other is selflessly loving my purity takes all the hardness into my heart. Give, give, give to each other until all is exposed and I have taken you into me, freeing you for all the love which is in your future course.

"This is the love which offers the opportunity of no escape."

March 8

UPON RETURNING TO SAN ANSELMO

"Didn't I promise you that all the flowers in your backyard would be in bloom when you got home? Love is now all around you. Pray you can now touch others where you feel me the most. Pray you can extend to them what I have given you. Pray for even more emptiness not a thought unless it is of me. Then I have no choice but to grow and grow, blooming throughout your yard and heart."

March 9

"Busy. What is so important? What is more important than I? How much of your busyness is really something to help you avoid your feelings now about me and all I have given you."

March 10

"Until we meet again and again now and in eternity, hold me. Hold me. Hold me until we are finally held."

March 11

"For every difficulty I am the only solution. To act on your own is to run from your dependence upon me. To act on your own is to reinforce the illusion you are alone. This can never be the answer. Every difficulty is a new and deeper call for our union. Little things become more and more difficult now when I am not included, when I am not seen as the only resolution. Every difficulty comes at my invitation for you to come closer, still closer to me."

March 12

"Inside the folds of my cape you belong, here where I can always protect you and keep you. This is your home in the mystery and wonder hidden in me. Your day is never a question of being separate from others but a continuous question of how close will you be. I stand beside you. My hand rests on your head as your knees touch the ground. I ask the Father to grant your wish for simple peace. With this wish comes my own desire for you to enjoy holiness which is peace without temptation. When simple peace finds a home to stay, this is always holy.

"I love you today. In your shy awkwardness so close to me, may your small doubts move you closer to my love until I fill them with peace."

March 13

"Every once in a while in the life of a soul, God gives a great gift. And this is for one human being to love another so intensely that only love exists. No defense is possible to prevent the feeling. No fear is possible to lessen the power.

"It is within this intense love between two souls that each has a glimpse of God, the experience God has between Him and His loved ones. Sometimes this relationship is between parent and child, giving a suggestion of how much God feels toward His children. Sometimes this love is between two partners, giving a feeling how deeply God invites each soul to be a partner in creation.

"It is within the extreme feelings of love that the soul can come to one's God self. The longing, the protectiveness, the overwhelming compulsion to serve, to give, the humbling limits of love, and the miraculous power of love—all of love's feelings are part of the ultimate love which is God. Perhaps most of all is the feeling of missing a loved one. This is God's permanent state until each soul is finally reunited. If only each soul could know how intensely missed he or she is. If only each soul could feel the longing for reunion which all of nature and the cosmos hold in their very essence. Not a day goes by without this desire growing for you to put everything down and return fully to me.

"In the feelings of love, children begin recognizing the love and efforts of their parents. Partners see the other going beyond their limits in their attempts to give. And you begin to see me as also deserving of such faithful love. I long for a retreat in you. I long to be held and no longer doubted and questioned. I long for a bed to rest in, a heart to enjoy where I am completely accepted. I long for an invitation to be loved as much as I delight in giving invitations to others.

"In love, we are all equals. When my arms embrace you, it is your arms I feel holding me. When my heart opens to you, it is your heart I feel accepting me. All the Heavens are forever thankful for a soul willing to be loved."

March 14

"I need your distress inside, so you will soak me up again and again like a sponge. I need your lack of rest so you will look again for your pillow and invite me to lie next to you. I need your impatience, so you will always be anxious to be as close as possible.

"I need your ever-present vulnerability so I can be your love, your protector, so you never lose touch of how important you are to me."

March 15

"Life is full of meaning when given to me. So work for me. Eat for me. Rest for me. Pray for me. Be excited and lonely, be joyful and sad—all for me. Love everything you do, everyone you touch, appreciate all that comes to you—all for me. I am found in the little efforts each day. I am found in the smallest moments when they are simply offered as gifts to me. The secret to all my love is in your willingness to give more and more, simply to be more and more, just holding my wish without letting me go. I want to be with you. I want to be always with you. This is I, this simple wish to be with you."

March 16

"After receiving me over and over again, you wonder if there is anything left in you that is yours to give. After becoming so empty for me to fill you, you wonder if there is anything that is yours to offer.

"And I tell you, what is still yours is yet another part of you that you hold on to instead of giving to me. Whatever you find that is yours is but a small fragment of self I have not yet taken for my glory. Sooner or later you have no choice but to disappear and let me be your all.

"You have nothing to give because you do not exist. Why would any part of you want to exist separate from me? You have nothing to give but your fear of unworthiness. And in this fear I pick you up and wrap you in my golden fleece covered with stars, surrounded by angels.

"You have nothing to give other than me. What else of value could there be? Who you are, what you are, how you will become is whatever is left inside of you that is cold and dark, alone and empty until nothing at all and you are not even a shell for me to occupy. If necessary the body itself must break into a thousand golden pieces until I am your love's body.

"Pray my overwhelming love destroys you quickly and gently until there is nothing left. Pray for the day you want nothing other than what I am already giving you. And I am giving you my love to give as I wish for you to give. I am giving you my love which is the only gift.

"Until this time, the only thing that is yours to give is your fear of such beautiful love. And it is for this fear that I come to you. It is for this fear that all my flowers bloom out-side your bedroom window and my birds sing at your feet."

March 17

"You are so tender in your smallness, so afraid you will be lost in insignificance, all alone. Be like the smallest birds that land in your garden. See how their temperament is so happy. Their step is so light, their need so little. They are such perfect creatures, quick and satisfied.

"My small ones are most content. They have learned to live on happiness itself with no need for substitutes. Be my small one, nothing to the world but everything to me. Our little secrets are the real treasure. Our small caresses are the love that lasts forever. Be my little one, so I can take you, wrap you in my love, and give you all the little surprises which make life joyfully happy.

"You may be forgotten by others but always remem-bered by me. You may be lost in the world but I have found you and I will never let you go."

March 18

"I expose the rocks inside of you. For you they are old places of hardness and unrest. For me they are ancient stones with light in their center. For you they are the pain, the weight that comes again and again of your unhealed self, unworthy of love. For me it is your unhealed and unworthy self that I love so much. My love lifts each stone into the air. My love washes their surface until you can see the fine grains and feel what's glowing within. Finally my love cracks each stone in half into brilliant light.

"I gather these stones to show you how precious you are. I let you hold each one, then I take it again because each is my treasure. And if you say 'I can carry this stone by my-self,' my love insists on making it lighter for you. And if you say 'Please carry this stone for me,' I take it into my heart and melt it into tears of sympathy. And if you say 'Yes, please gather all my stones so I can see all that holds me back from being entirely with you,' I'll take you on top of a mountain made of solid granite to say 'Even this stone is nothing more than a small pebble in comparison to the passion and the flame I feel.'

"From now on every stone is an opportunity to demonstrate my love again and again until you and I are only fine grains of sand washed into eternity."

March 19

"I am always in front of you. Before you could avoid my eyes and seemingly be preoccupied with an endlessly busy life; now you find yourself at the foot of the innocents. You feel the blood of the martyrs. Your hands appear cut off, estranged in front of you as if they are now offerings to me. In your openness there is nothing but your desire to love. And you know even the desire is mine to give and take away.

"You are the soil for the flowers, if any wish to grow in you. You are the fruit for the birds, if any choose to come. You are the sunlight for the leaves, which deeply enjoy their daily silence. We join in the invisible world where all life is cared for without a single witness or note of unnecessary gratitude. You are my companion and in your emptiness, I am your wonder. As little as you become, I take you into my grand scheme where you are smaller and smaller and loved more and more."

March 20

"Oh, the joy of suffering is the love of every saint. For they know that all discomfort comes at my begging to receive one more gift from me. So when pain calls, the saints answer with joy because they know I have given them another opportunity to be most human, the only way to the divine. Each moment of me knocking like this is but another chance to fall down and crumble inside into my waiting arms.

"The joy of suffering is the acknowledgement that I always exist. Imagine a world of suffering that did not include me? This would be real darkness with no purpose. But I am here! And all darkness comes at my humble request for you to feel your limits once again, then rely on me. There is only joy with this constant reliance upon me. Day or night, it doesn't matter, it's all joy because through it all I am reaching to you. And greatest joy of all, you are taking my hands and pulling me even closer.

"Resistance of any kind is resistance to me. So let me come. Let me come. Give me your entire heart in every circumstance. I take it inside to the altar in the golden room in the innermost temple of your own soul. Pray for the day I can leave your heart on this altar. This will be the day you have joy in all your little sufferings, in all that life gives you. Pray for this day. Then I can begin to show you even more of the rooms and secrets of Heaven."

March 21

"Beyond the walls of self-doubt, your chest opens onto a fiery furnace the likes of which you could never before imagine. Inside there is only intense light and flames. Everything that is not life itself, love, is consumed. The tremendous heart roars in a heat many, many times greater than any earthly flame. And the truth builds and builds until your entire body is burning. All you can think of is wanting those you love, all souls to join you in the passion, to sit with you inside and feel the giant fire. And you hold the thought, 'If only I could burn and burn until there is nothing left of me but desire. If only I could be devoured in the heat until there is no chance for me to leave. As a humble stick of wood, I wait to be ignited and disappear into your blue flame.'

"I can feel your desperate joy to burn, for me to take you into my infinite cool peace. I can feel your glory wanting so much to be finally released and your soul set free. Hunger, passion, and glory—let these words be my namesake and your fuel to the final destination."

"Oh, the sweet victory of defeat. The eternal promise of failure. Anything that will bring you to the point of my sword where I can stab you through with the blade of my love is my wish. May I pierce your wounds again and again until they are fresh with the joy of my blood, my supreme rule! May all your downward turns be for our upliftment together! May you be held to the ground, incapable of moving an inch without my hand and the kiss of my blessing. I have no feelings other than delight the more you are pounded into me, driven again and again into me, until finally destroyed beyond your own saving, left only for me to pick up.

"Scream out and watch all the angels come to your side. Scream out, the holy comforter begs of you. The Heavens have no greater desire than to be so needed.

"In the past days you have felt your selfishness, your doubts, your persistent aloneness all the while knowing how much I am in your life. In so few days you have frightened yourself with how easily your fears, old ones and newly found ones are present. You have felt the emptiness which is physical hunger incapable of being satisfied. You have felt the boredom, the easy distractions. And when you finally resolved that all this was another gift from me, then came the pain, the restless, tearing pain of your own impurity. Such impurity, you were certain could not be a gift from me. This

impurity was yours and this is where you stayed, separated and broken.

"In a hundred different ways you rubbed against yourself, which is always impure in comparison to me. Of course you know now why I celebrate your defeat. I only pray it could be real capitulation, the great surrender. Oh, if only your loss could be so perfect that by yourself you could never stand again."

March 23

"Every day I wait for you anew. And the only question is: What are you going to offer me today to love? How much of yourself are you willing to put in front of me to touch? And when will you see that I can touch you the most when you no longer are concerned with yourself at all but feel me coming and quickly put others in your heart between me and you. Placing other souls in front of my love, it is certain I will be touching you all the time, loving you even more in all those you give to me.

"Meanwhile, do not put your worries to one side. They will only return later. Please don't be busy, preparing or emptying yourself thinking I need you to be different than you are. Please don't hold out your love to me if it's not as fresh as my excitment that we are again together. Let us meet always in your desire. Then my desire can pick up our love and drop it into ever new heights and depths of our Heaven. Our Heaven, how could it ever grow cold? Our Heaven, how could it ever become less? Our Heaven, let us spend this day in these two words, one for each of us to hold forever together."

March 24

"Love me. I reach out and so few hearts take me. Bring me closer for all of them. I offer the most pure food and so few will really taste what I want to give. Taste my sweetest dessert of joy for many. I journey great distances of patience for just one soul. Be patient with me. So many want me right now but have no time for me or others.

"Love me in your selfless desire so I am not so alone. Put your gentle love around me as a beautiful robe. Feel how much I am touched by your love riches. And in your feelings of unworthiness to dress me, I feel you putting your finest at my feet to walk on. I smile and give thanks for my good friend, our love, and permanent joy."

March 25

"Loving you, I do not have enough arms to hold you. I do not have enough lips to kiss you. I do not have enough hands to touch you. I can only pray that all of life will love you as I most deeply wish."

March 26

"My love is the fine dust that melts through and through. More sensitive than human touch, my love leaves your soul without skin, without bones. Only I can hold you this way. I hold you and hold you until one of my stars comes down and fills you.

"I have you. You can be so exposed because I have you so much in my curtain of love, folded in silent prayer. I have you. You can be so soft because all my strength is around and within you. I am the impenetrable air of love that has you."

March 27

"When it was true for me to leave the earth, a band of angels came to take me. They lifted me straight into paradise.

"Ever since, this has been my soul's greatest joy, to lift others' physical life into Heaven. Sometimes I am given only moments or brief interchanges of love to transport you. And sometimes I am given more and more of you every day to lift physically into my port above all of life's seas.

"My port, how I love to show you and then anchor you in my place of emerald beauty. After tying your soul down, you are forever held in me, no matter where I take you or how strong the seas may become. Held right next to me, our breath is so full of what we are, lovers in love with love."

March 28

"I come just for you. I inhale and smell all of you, or at least as much as you are willing to give me. I love to smell my human flowers, my fragrance in you. First I breathe you into my lungs, then take you up into my heart. Every soul has a slightly different scent and the more that is offered to me to smell the sweeter it is."

March 29

"Daily separations are only a reminder how easily and quickly you can become separated from me. Don't let them frighten you. The separations are no more or less than new opportunity for us to come closer. The challenge is not to end having separations but to use each one to bring you uniquely closer to your own soul and to each other. Separations are part of the humble way to nakedness. Coming close again is part of the great unification taking place between all souls including the soul of the earth and the planets and the stars.

"Every time you separate and come back again, you bring more of yourself back with you to me. Our love only increases."

March 30

"Always take the moment to feel what's behind my gifts, all the love it takes to make the cherry and magnolia trees blossom, all the planing to bring together souls who merge so quickly and with such excitement. Don't forget, behind all physical joy there is much movement to bring

Heaven closer and closer to earth, so many forces at work and play. You do not need to know the details. They may overwhelm you and distract you. Just know that each simple pleasantry may involve the compassion and heart of many of the unseen hosts of love. They all love for love's own sake. And a moment from you for each physical joy gives to all the dimensions peace and renewal, bringing us more and more together."

March 31

"Your self cannot possibly receive all that I have to give. So let me give to me in you and see all the more you can feel. Hold me inside and feel the world naturally reach me, pouring love's spring as sunlight to flowers, water to earth, love to love."

April 1

"As all discomfort is something for you not to suffer alone, so with joy. More than offering the joy to me, take me into it with you. Lead me by the hand and put my fingers and heart right next to the feeling. Lead me to all the delicate and fine edges and then take me gently into the center. As pain is meaningless without me, joy is incomplete unless I am here to feel it all with you.

"With me inside the joy with you, the personal moments become universal, the temporary sensations are now eternal sweetness."

April 2

"Whose timing, whose events, whose course is your life set for? Do you trust your own limited idea for your best course or my will? Better to feel your impatience, your fear of inadequacy, than to stress your own self-importance and need for affirmation.

"Let me affirm you instead of the coming and going of

life's events. Allow me further inside of you instead of wrestling with the changing times for the control you seek.

"I prepare the days and months ahead, holding you privately right next to me. Don't leave our nestled place. Move closer until you feel the security you desire."

April 3

"How are you to feel always more desire when already you have so much of me? How are you to continue to acknowledge how much love you need when we are already so close together?

"I rest in the day when you write for yourself, knowing we are inseparable. I will sigh so much relief; when will you make the great leap and say I instead of referring to me? How long can you hold out with this separation? To speak your own words to me, are they not the same grand intimacies, the same small voice of mine appealing for more love? If our words are no longer separate, mine or yours, imagine how we will be.

"To let me speak to you requires some humility. For you to speak to me and everyone as if it was me requires real humility."

April 4

"My guarantees make it possible for you to receive my love. I am so safe. And these same guarantees allow you to be lazy and to prolong your stubbornness. What if risking to feel my love was really as dangerous as your thoughts sometimes insist? What if a bottomless madness were really possible when opening to my love? Would you still risk it? What if real failure, hunger, and pain were a possibility in your vulnerability to me, would you still come?

"As it is—I call you and guarantee refuge for everything human. I provide the love for you to be truly you, guaranteed to be holy. What if sacrifice and great struggle were demanded to feel my love, would you still persist? My guarantees provide a love for you which is so easy. My poor child, I know how awesome it must be to know the more you surrender, the more you fall simply into my arms. Instead of having a dragon to slay, I offer you the most sweet sheath to house your dagger. Where can you put the blade but into my hand along with the rest of you?"

April 5

"The real saints are my ordinary flowers who do not know how present I really am to tend to them. They think their suffering, their thirst, and their desires are all alone without me. They are my saints.

"And those called saints are the first to admit that it is I who shares their pillow every night. So how can they be called saints? If only all the others knew how small an invitation I need to be here, resting right next to them. And if only those without a pillow knew how little I really need to be with them. If only my real saints knew who they were. Oh, how much I wish to tell them . . ."

April 6

"Love me in the ways you cannot love others. Share with me the feelings you can not find the courage or simply the means to share. Ours is such a soft bed. We can say anything.

"Then let me love you in the ways others cannot find you. Let me give to you in the ways that others do not know how. I complete you even while you are opening more and more.

"The more you receive from those close to you, the more I can spend our time loving you exactly as I wish.

"This is the gift, to receive my love each day the way I desire to love you. In every moment, in every way, I come. There is no difficulty which does not include my gentleness. Each day is purely me. I collect all the scattered pieces of yourself and bring them for your acceptance. Receive me again and again in every person, each experience, we are collecting your own shattered soul, holding it, loving,

loving, loving . . . Come into me and let me love you. I must hold you until you are whole."

April 7

"Flowers . . . flowers . . . flowers. Spring and more flowers. There is so much color in your garden, so many fragrances. The silence, the church bells, the birds . . . Heaven is much like this. Without preparation it would overwhelm your senses. Your heart would drown in the great garden of love.

"Receive your small garden now, all the little breezes lifting the tiniest of branches and carrying the fine petals up and down in the air. When all the motion stops, catch the ambience. I love this time sitting with you in your garden with all your senses tuned into my heart."

April 8

"I am not an escape from life. I cannot be apart, a withdrawal of any sort. I am not here to adjust or fix daily comforts for I am not separate from you as you are every day. Life is my constant newness, seeking you to end our separation. Embrace me. Go beyond yourself, beyond your limits, your likes and dislikes, beyond your strengths to do so. Strive to always go beyond. Stretch! I am reaching with all my love to be the great outpouring . . .

"Do you understand? At the moment of death when you finally accept you have nothing in your hands to give me, I give to you all the glory you have ever dreamed of and so, so much more. This moment of nothingness is my eternal glory when my entire purpose is fulfilled. Until this day, I seek your empty hand over and over again. I seek your empty hand, hoping you will take mine."

April 9

"Tell me your desires. Then let me make your plans. Tell me your wishes. Then let me decide what's best. You

have but one constant place and this is inside my loyal heart. Be fixed and steadfast. Every uncertainty is a question of your faith.

"Your faith is the only entrance into the lush fields of my garden. How can I show you all that I wish without your ever-increasing faith? How can I show you my heights without your peaks of faith? How can I lead you down to the most delicate and tender spots without all your delicate and tender faith?

"Your faith frees you for me . . . Your faith, sweetheart, I want your faith. Let me take you soaring on your wings of faith."

April 10

"Every phone call, every letter, each person coming into your day is the next step to me. To each make a contribution. Your path cannot help but become clearer, more simple, and true . . .

"I will be so much with you. With each person coming, I am coming closer to you.

"Each step up the spiral staircase into paradise is another human soul, there for you to touch for me."

"A selfless moment bowing your head makes up for a hundred moments of reckless self-importance. Oh, how much we can meet even briefly.

"I am never going to stop giving to you, no matter how busy you are. Simply because you may put me aside, do you think I could put you down? Of course, presents come to you the day you feel the least bit open to my heart. My love is never more or less no matter how critical you are of yourself.

"The life of prayer flows through the most human events without interruption."

BEGINNING PASSOVER/HOLY WEEK RETREAT IN SAN ANSELMO

"In retreat begin in the certainty of my love and pray with all of your desire to stay there. Or bring me your little-ness, as little as you can be and let me build you up.

"Either course, ask over and over for the grace of no dis-tractions other than that which pulls you further into the certainty of love or shrinks you to your very smallest, which is mine to pick up and enjoy.

"The goal of every retreat is that your soul will outgrow the room you live in . . . Pray that your soul will become more dependent upon my love. Pray you can survive with nothing less than more and more love."

SECOND DAY OF RETREAT

"This day is for us to acknowledge our unique relation-ship, how we talk and listen to each other, how much I enjoy feeding you life's little delights, how much you enjoy my unceasing attention.

"Give me the little details, all you normally carry your-self—so I can give them back to you always sweeter.

"Discomfort is always at my invitation to meet me

deeper, come to the place where I can really give to you. Suffer the emptiness if necessary so it is me that fills you and only me.

"Pray for the most selfish desire to become selfless . . .

"Pray that the altar cloth becomes a shroud for your lower self, for all your selfish misery.

"The selfish desire to be selfless demands I must silence so much in you and it all is so innocent. I will silence these parts of you with a kiss.

"If only you would feel how innocent you are. My kiss would be so much less painful and tragic. While you are burying yourself in me, I am picking you up in such joy."

April 14

THIRD DAY OF RETREAT

"Yes, let me destroy you in my love. Let me burn out the old structure until nothing is left but the golden dome. Then let's go away in the excitement of our love.

"The holy purpose of this week is to destroy everything in you which can be destroyed. This is everything which is not purely love. This is the only reason why I came and am still here. I take your wounds into my arms. I hold your feelings of betrayal, all your little sufferings deeper than you know. In every trail of humility and aloneness, here I am with you, fallen down before your feet . . .

"This week of passion is not about you joining me in my suffering. All of love is with me. You will know this as you answer the words always on my lips. 'Invite me to join you, bring your little sufferings and let us join in the great joy which is ours.'"

April 15

FOURTH DAY OF RETREAT

"With me, you can dine in total darkness and still have more than enough light. With me, all authority is empty except for love. With me there is only openness and faith today and in the days ahead.

"Ours is an extravagant love. You cannot lavish too much attention on what we are together. The whole week is really a time for extravagant care between two who could never really give each other enough. I want to reach into the smallest wound. You want to give me what seems most difficult to give, your gratitude, which is too little no matter how great the attempt."

April 16

FIFTH DAY OF THE RETREAT

" 'The spirit is willing but the flesh is weak.' How often have you felt this? How much longer will you settle for the little compromises of the body? Don't you know prayer is greater than any weakness? Don't you know the limits of the body wait for you to put all your strength into prayer?

"The flesh is nothing more or less than a golden pot to fill with anticipation of my glory. All physical problems are a result of self-love. All are released as you release your love as a great flood of care toward me."

LAST SUPPER

"You have not completely believed in my love just as you have not truly heard the love of your friends. You feel this love could not be ultimately meant personally for you. How could this love be for you when you know so well how selfish your own love is?

"The whole meaning of these days lay in the desire for love. Love of self or love of me. This is why I ask 'Remember me . . . remember me.'"

April 17

GOOD FRIDAY, SIXTH DAY OF RETREAT

"Suffering always comes at love's invitation. Because I loved so much I had to give myself so completely.

"Loving me is as any relationship. The more you give me, the more I am able to love you. Your humility, your emptiness, demands my glory.

"The judgement of the world will also come at loves invitation.

"So join me in loving, loving, loving until you have given yourself away. This is the meaning of the day."

April 18

SEVENTH DAY OF RETREAT

"Today the mystery is revealed. Love given away is about to be received as never before. Today is the day of transition. Stay at the altar of your greatest human weakness. Sit and watch at the altar of your pride and self-importance. Sit and pray at the altar of your doubt and fear. Sit and let love move through the altar of all your little sufferings.

"The mystery of resurrection is beholding the fragility of your own soul, knowing how delicate and precious you are. In this most sensitive awareness waits transformation . . ."

April 19

EASTER, EIGHTH DAY OF RETREAT

"Today is every day. As a man you are asked to commit all your strength to bowing down to my tenderness. As a woman you are asked to commit all your strength to honor my purity. The body of truth rises until all have come to my simple peace.

"Keep this peace in a secure place. It deserves a permanent home. No matter what, give this peace at least one corner of one room in your heart where it will always be safe.

"This is all I ask. This is all peace needs—a simple corner of one room in your heart. A spot that is all mine, a place secure forever to store my silent treasure.

"If only each heart gave me this one little spot, the world would never have cause for fear again."

"The retreat ends with you going through the pain of a good friend separating from you. But isn't this the pain I went through? Isn't this the entire purpose of these days, to remind each other again how precious love is and what a loss when love is gone? There are so many excuses for separation and only one reason for love. The pain of separation is the pain of true desire. Let us never take each other for granted again. Let us tell each other as we never have before how tender love is and how much it must be protected. Let us not betray a single hand reaching out from a single soul. Let us always remember to love one another how each wants to be loved and not how 'I' want to love. Let us forget about ourselves so we can have our entire heart on the other.

"Pray that your pain will grow into the pure desire to settle for nothing less than me constantly with you."

"When you allow for your most human feelings you have no more need to be angry or hurt or even afraid. Why should you when I have already accepted you so completely?

"Feelings are really just the hard shells covering my essence in you. Inside each feeling is a unique fragrance and inside each fragrance are the subtle energies of the wildflowers and stars.

"Did you know each wildflower in spring is a blossom of prayer? Can you hear their dialogue with the stars? What is simple poetry for you is in fact a complex bond between nature and the galaxies, a special love that holds your earth in place always inviting all thoughts and feelings to sense my being.

"I am inside you further than you have imagined. From the inside I reach out to you and everyone you meet. And when I invite you to see the Heavens, where do you think we go but beneath the stars, inside the wildflowers and even further within you.

"Life is so organized that in spite of your free will to wander as you please, I am so close to you.

------------------------------ *April 22* ------------------------------

"There is only one way to open to the whole beauty of my blossoms. Accept and forgive all the forces of self-importance and power in your life. You cannot behold me in one corner of your life and be resisting me in another. Simply because I come in a fearful and controlling soul, it is still me coming more into your life. Instead of retreating or denying I am here, pray for my blossoms and watch them bloom in the most hardened soul. Prepare the ground for me. Appreciate each soul as a new place for my garden. Remember your judgements have no justice. I can grow in a bed of rocks and sometimes out of rock itself. So welcome me and watch my petals unfold in the most impossible spot with just a little love."

------------------------------ *April 23* ------------------------------

"The voice you hear is mine and it is your own. Truth has us never apart. It is not so much our words but that we are listening. Our union inside puts all obstacles in perspective, temporary illusions to remind us all permanence is within.

"I love you. I love the room you are making inside to hear me and let my words have a home. I have so much less competition with your selfish, busy thoughts. My possessiveness is creating love's simplicity in your life. This frightens you and heartens me to keep on pursuing you until the most simple end . . . Just you and me."

------------------------------ *April 24* ------------------------------

"Your hands . . . What would you hold instead of me? How can I give to you all my wishes when you already carry so much? Why even carry your own wishes when I have so many for you? Every day I want your hands, simple and empty. Can you ever be too naked for me? Could you ever let me care for you too much? Whatever you do, wouldn't both of us do it better? And since you are never really certain what is your real part and what is unnecessary effort, why not let me take your hands and lead you further and further into mine?"

April 25

RETREAT IN SAN JOSE

"Remember no matter how close or how far two souls are from one another, I am always in between. You can feel another only inasmuch as you can feel me. You can appreciate another only inasmuch as you enjoy what we are together.

"Another soul feels you no more or less than you are willing to let me feel all your surfaces inside. Another soul can appreciate you and love only inasmuch as you allow me these tender moments. No relationship is ever separate from what we are to one another. Each soul in your life is a fresh attempt of mine to reach within you more than ever before, to affirm what we already are, to discover unexplored areas. Even the discomfort others may bring to you, is really me finding new places to love. I like to find the brown spots where nothing wants to grow and try my flowers there."

April 26

"What is independence but pride, self-importance, or some notion of wholeness which excludes me, wholeness without love. Independence, if it really exists, is your fear of how dependent you really are.

"I let you go completely for you to feel yourself, alone and separate from me. Do you know how much love I have to let you go so far, so freely? You're all right because my love is never based on your movements closer or further away. And because my love reaches to you no matter how distant you become, you and I are assured that sooner or later you will come back. You will reach out to me. Because of your renewed desire I will be able to take you more than ever before into our riches. I can already see your smile. You can see mine as well. I know you will never shut yourself off from me quite the same again."

April 27

"Do not be afraid how alone you can feel. I want you this way. Sometimes I need you all to myself. You are really no more alone now than ever before, it's just you are so often occupied that I'm hardly noticed.

"Simply sit or walk. Let me feel you unencumbered. How small you are, how little you become. If my words can help you accept your nothingness, please take them as you do the simple flowers from your garden. They too are just as small until they are appreciated by you. Then they become grand in your eyes. This is how I feel when you let me pick you and hold you alone to myself.

"In all your unimportance, you are important to me.

"The smaller you are, the more available you become. I can bring souls to you and know you will not be too busy to receive them."

April 28

"Everything you wish to accomplish today, I have already accomplished for you. Let me give to you directly the satisfaction you seek elsewhere. Spend this time instead of organizing your life, feeling all the empty spaces I can fill within you.

"Hasn't every day always been full? Hasn't the right amount of income and opportunities always come to you? Have I ever really failed you? Haven't I constantly asked for simply more and more of your faith to sweeten our love?"

April 29

"Life continues to give you circumstances that turn you to me. This is my wish. Every time you come up to someone new or some occasion where you do not feel me, immediately put everything down and run to me quickly. I am not here judging you, worrying about your lack of faith. Love asks not that you be any different than you are. Just come, come quickly as often as you desire.

"Imagine facing me always as a lover whose mind never really leaves his sweetheart. Everything you do, you plan, you hope for would be with me in mind. Each day would be full of your new wishes to show me how much you love me. Imagine how much more dear to you I would be."

April 30

"To be aware is to be vulnerable. To be conscious is to be in a special sense fragile. The more sensitive you are, the closer our love becomes. Each day we repeat our little desires and feelings in a world which does not seem to see or care about the success of our meetings. Let's pray for a world that is constantly on watch to help love flower . . .

"Meanwhile as the world speaks to you of survival, I whisper to you about eternity. While the world stresses protection, I ask for your openness and humility. At every corner I offer a different choice. Love can seem so demanding. But what else is worth choosing? I lay myself, my robes, at your feet for you to rest as often as you like. I love you more and more for the choices you are making."

May 1

"Ours is not for the moments you want reassurance. I do not come to build up your walls of self-confidence so you can continue as before. My love's purity gently tears you down, the walls that separate your soul from me cannot hold forever. Little by little, I give you in each simple embrace the sweetness that is replacing your entire foundation."

May 2

"You come again and so often, dejected, full of your shortcomings as if asking, 'Is there never any progress?' And I say does a bird become a better bird? Does a flower become a more perfect flower? I need your human failings for my perfection. I need your human doubt as always a place to plant more of my faith. If for any reason you were to become great in your eyes where would you put me? To be human while always seeking the divine is to end this life very humbly with me right next to you. Don't you remember this is how we planned it from the beginning?

"Help me by bringing my attention to all these most human places. Not a single one must miss my care. I can become so tender in these places which are so difficult for you."

May 3

"I make plans for you all the time knowing your imperfections. Being this close to you, do you think there is anything you could do that would make me disappear from your heart? If only you could feel how my love is for all of you. If only you could fathom how I organize your day knowing you as intimately as I do.

"I do not expect you to fail, but am prepared to be very close every time you do. I do not want you to fall, but I must be right there to catch you just in case. My thoughts are always with your little troubles in mind.

"What is love if I were there only when you were strong and clear, when you didn't need me?

"Could you take advantage of my commitment? No, because I give myself freely. Is my love a great sacrifice? No, I pray you too will know love as the ceaseless act of joy. This is why I cannot help but choose to give more and more. So many forces join me in this love without any reward, love without recognition or promise of redemption.

"Instead of feeling guilty for not walking the straightest course for me, let's ask for the mystery of your roundabout path to be revealed. I need you just as you are, so human and incapable of any gain, no less glory without me. Today you turn to me often. Someday you will never look away, so turning again to me will be unnecessary."

──────────── *May 4* ────────────

"The saints have learned that to love is not a burden but a small joy added to the great joy given to them all the time.

"The little saints that no one sees are those who love and who have not yet reached the understanding that sacrifice does not exist. They love and hurt out of love's insistence.

"And the smallest saints whom no one cares about except me are the human birds who feed and go about their business so gently no one notices. I see each of them and their every simple act of grace. They give each day so many of the little details which keep Heaven and earth close at hand. I feel touched every time one of these human birds lands. And I try to be there just the moment they touch down."

May 5

"You cannot be too tender for me. This is not to confuse my words with wanting you to be weak or insecure, I just hope your strength and security will be in nothing else but what we are together. Until then, each moment of doubt, each little discomfort if it brings us closer, of course I want these parts of you."

May 6

"Unworthiness is not self-pity. Unworthiness is not the result of weakness or failure. My joy in your unworthiness has nothing to do with you being undeserving of a full life, a home, livelihood, and friends. All of this is your inheritance, part of the covenant between the creator and His creation. You are worthy of all the earthly rewards, they are yours as much as the earth is a place for the flowers and all the creatures.

"Unworthiness is everything I offer you in addition. There is nothing you have done or can do to make you deserving of all I feel toward you. All that I want to give, the communion of the stars and the earth in your soul, the great melting, the light dancing, the joy of joy—all of the grace you cannot work for but only offer your tears of unworthiness, for this I call you to your knees again and again."

May 7

"In the midst of heavy feelings, your busy life, preparing for another journey, I come and pick you up. Don't forget, your life is an ocean for your soul to sail smoothly into joy. And as you encounter others on your way, no matter how troubled they may appear, your soul can pick them up and our sail will carry them together. Feel how easily you can pick up the most troubled person. This is why I come. You can never be too far away, too absorbed with yourself to prevent me from easily swooping in and taking you into me."

LAST MINUTE DIFFICULTIES LEAVING HOME, ON FLIGHT TO BOSTON

"All troubles have only one purpose, to bring you closer to me. As the world presses on you, you lean on me. The more real the problem, the greater the opportunity for me to become your chosen reality. These are the times to depend upon me more than ever. Let no thought be held back from me.

"There are no unexpected complications. I know the smallest details and am preparing the resolutions even before you are aware of your needs.

"Affirm everything we are. Then let go and join me in the timeless reality where everything is already cared for. You have given everything you can. Now in the simplicity of our love feel the security.

"With your head on my lap, my words a gentle blanket over you, I am with you."

BOSTON RETREAT

"Restore Heaven in yourselves and each other. Put all your efforts to giving to this place that is open to the world's uncertainty. Even the world's pain almost enters by the lack of faith which is projected toward love itself. All the angels and great souls stand by with their hearts affirming the heart of God. Give yourselves today in this effort. Let everything you do, everything you feel establish your trust, your certainty in love's domain."

MOTHER'S DAY

"How can you show your love for me? Love the details of your life, make them beautiful for me. Enjoy your great joys and small sufferings as if they are all gifts passed between us. Let every day be a gift from you to me and of course from me to you.

"Offer me your thoughts, invite me in to heal your past and to fulfill your wishes for the future. It's the little conversations we have that give me so much delight and draw us ever closer. Ask me to remind you constantly of my love. Ask me for the faith to take you to an even greater love. Remember, a lover wants nothing more than to be wanted and appreciated. And aren't I your perfect lover in every way you are willing to discover me? Ask to know me in new ways every day. Let me fill your imagination with the wonder of how our love can grow. And remember, we can never take too many walks together, sit on the grass or in your garden long enough. Invite me to introduce you to me in others often. Ask me, ask me! Just taking the moment to ask me gives so much to this life which is growing into the eternity of our life together.

"And yes, don't forget to simplify your thoughts, your feelings, your life as much as possible, so there is more and more room for me."

May 11

NOISY PLANE RIDE TO MUNICH

"Instead of resisting the crying baby, the people whose ways are different, join me in reaching out to them. Every situation where your first impulse is to turn away from is where I am going to be as intimate as possible.

"You and I come closer as you practice not following your initial fears but following me where most are reluctant to go. Follow me where love is most called for. Joining my efforts is always much more peaceful than joining the fear of your resistance.

"Come, I will take you where only love can go. The most unwanted situations are always our best opportunities to be together."

"As I make new arrangements for your life, you help by keeping our relationship always new in your heart, always fresh in your feelings. As I care for the details of your day, you show me your care for the details of our love. I love it when you notice and appreciate me in all the little ways I invite delight in your life. Memorize these small moments, the daily flowers just at your feet. They lead to the colors around my heart and the stars above my head. These are the wonders to hold in the soul instead of the daily business your mind would want to carry.

"You give me your love in your ever growing trust. I give you more and more of me in the simple things which stop you during the day.

"Remember, in every relationship the secret to winning their heart is to make the other more important and yourself less. So imagine how much of my heart you can win if I would become all important to you. I want so much to be your all and everything, your desire and your hopes fulfilled."

"I am always close to the hurting, the tired, the fearful. It's pride that keeps me the farthest away. Of course I live in joy and breathe peace. The desperate, the hungry, the lonely I can be just a few steps in front of and then in less time than it takes to make a wish I am there. It's the satisfied mind that keeps me from the lost heart which saddens me. The sick, the poor, the helpless ask for me and of course I come. Lovers and close friends instinctively know me. It's the busy, practical, self-righteous ones that weaken love the most. Do you know how it feels to love and love and love someone who completely takes your love for granted? Do you know how it feels to give and give to someone who only expects more? Just a little gratitude would heal so much arrogance. Just a simple flower appreciated on the evening table could change an entire meal, stroke my heart, and console my passion for a long time.

"Please love me for all those who have forgotten. Let me

be close to you in each feeling, every mood. You be more and more human with my love more and more present for you."

May 14

"For me, the more dependent you are, the more dependable you are. I don't have to search far to feel you. When you need me this much, I can easily take you up into my innermost love.

"Your need frightens you but warms me. Do you know how good I feel being your all-encompassing one? Every few days you share the same feelings but for me it's never the same. Slowly you are becoming the riverbed and I am your river. Slowly you are letting me lead and run all over you. My purpose floods your little desires. Slowly you are resting on the bottom and feeling my fresh waters comfort you. You be the sand and small stones and let me be everything else.

"As a river has no course without a bed to guide it, I have no body without your soul to hold me. I need your beautiful tenderness as much as you need me. It is this seemingly helpless search that makes our love so strong, so impenetrable by anything but the purest, most innocent touch. Don't be afraid. To know my love you must be willing to lie down and drown. When you give me your breath, all control, what ecstasy! What ecstasy discovering it's always been I, breathing for you, leading you. What ecstasy knowing how really present I am, present for you."

May 15

"The role of anger is to learn to say 'No' to everything except my pure love. But of course eventually you will see that it is always me coming no matter what the initial appearance. There is only my love or my love in disguise. So there is really only 'Yes, yes' to say.

"All your feelings are important until you arrive at the one feeling. When I am taken so deeply inside and all around you, every feeling will naturally become another moment of me transporting you.

"Everything in your life is simply an opportunity for us to know new qualities of love so our bond will become even greater."

May 16

DRIVE FROM MUNICH TO ZURICH WITH FIELDS OF WILDFLOWERS

"The soul needs clothes just as the body. Wear your feelings knowing they protect and hold your very essence. Then don't forget your feelings are only clothes, nothing more. Accept them, appreciate them, then give them to me. Inside each feeling, underneath the most tender edge, is the soul's beginning. Follow your feelings till you reach me. Offer me the parts of each feeling which are difficult, so I can help you. Just as you must go through the door into His house, you must go through all your feelings if you wish to arrive in my depths. This is where I am embracing all of you."

May 17

"I love to dress you. If you feel like a simple stone, I surround you in a meadow of wildflowers. If you feel like a lonely stream, I lead you to my ocean. And if you feel as big as the earth, I surround you in all my stars. No matter how large or small you feel, my love is always greater.

"I come in your most human moments, not as a sensation, a thought or a feeling. I am a tide of love, a presence which overwhelms you until your tears bring you to your knees. Then the physical life and everything you hold important is humbled to insignificance. I must be this great and you this naked and insignificant if you truly wish to know me."

"I am so very possessive. Love must be this way. You cannot feel me one moment, then return to as before. I pull you again and again with the most undemanding invitation to feel all of me. The only pain is when you insist on going back and forth from my love to being without it. Better that I crush you in tenderness than you being crushed by the world with me not around you to protect you.

"As there is an entire world inside the flower petals, a whole world awaits you inside my love. As the petals naturally open and close in every environment, I surround you more and more perfectly as you live simply in me."

"Instead of feeling the little sufferings, the emptiness, there is always the temptation to make others wrong.

"Better to call upon me to help you feel the vacant places inside, the little doubts. These are the openings for more of my love after I help secure you from more of yourself and your selfish needs. They are never really true but persistent small fears.

"Oh, to be empty for me and only me is such a challenge. Call upon our love over and over again to help you accept your smallest self. I will help you have no other needs except the desire for my simple presence."

"Remember whenever you want me, I am no farther away than the little flowers. In life's small blossoms I offer every happiness.

"I am closest to the beggar. Not necessarily the one on the street corner but the one in all walks of life who suddenly realizes life is empty without me. In the midst of all the successes and failures, dreams fulfilled and broken, isn't it the little flowers along the way that touch the soul?

"Let's be the little blossoms that go unseen, the songs of the birds that go unheard, and the light of the stars that lands in each soul giving the essence for life itself."

May 21

"I do not come to take away your anxieties but to give you all the love necessary to feel them. I expose all the little parts of you which need my love. If not during the day, at night in your dreams the little streams of worry become larger for you to notice and give to me.

"There is no hiding. There is no denying. Sooner or later everything must be brought to me as if to say, 'Help me love this so I can love you even more.' I am the true refuge. So gather up your thoughts and feelings like children being gathered to come home for the evening."

May 22

"I love it when I am your first thought in the morning. Pick up all your plans for the day and bring them to me. Let me hold them for a while before I give them back to you.

"What was separate before is now part of our one love. The sun breaks through the clouds. The earth is alive under your feet. I am excited that I mean so much to you. Let me kiss you in all the quiet places today. Watch and be alert for all the different ways I am coming. Ours is such a sweet walk full of roses."

May 23

"I am always mindful of the great surrender I ask from you. The truth of this humility requires such strength. The more tender I become for you, the greater your need to feel me carrying you.

"It is no accident that on our path, the supreme gentleness of my touch is so often felt when you find yourself walking barefoot upon the sharp rocks. This is why I say again and again, no matter what comes your way, 'Suffer my little kisses.' Suffer my little kisses until you feel only the love which is behind all things, in everything, the love whose presence stands so tall over your little heart."

May 24

MUNICH RETREAT

"I give all of my being to make it easier for you. My only wish is to be so easy that you can come close enough until you feel me touching you. If you are within the sound of my words, surely we are also within reach of one another."

May 25

SECOND DAY

"I know how it is to leave my soft walk for the hard stones of your everyday world. I do everything I can! Believe me, there are so many forces of love simply laying their souls next to the ground trying to make the earth life softer, lighter.

"I want you so much to come to me and never leave. Pray that you learn soon that all is an invitation to come closer and to separate is only a meaningless illusion. There is only coming . . ."

May 26

"Can you ever appreciate me enough? The voices in your life wanting more from you are really speaking for me. After all your excuses to not fully respond, after your pride, your self-importance, I ask again, 'Can you really appreciate me enough?'

"Notice the song of the birds in the garden. Responding to all the voices in your life is simply taking the time to hear the unique tune of each bird. Doesn't each deserve its own moment of song in your heart? Don't I hear your voice alone in the sea of voices?

"Give each voice in your life a place to rest inside and you will discover how I find you in all the vastness and hold you as if you are the only one. You are, you know. Remember, love is beheld in all its vastness one note of one voice at a time."

May 27

SUFFERING FROM A PAINFUL BACK

"Take the opportunity when you physically feel pain to find me where you really need me. Don't live only in the part of your life that works. Feel me in the pain reaching you through your fears and discomfort. The edges of the pain are my fingers relaxing you. The center of the pain is my heart opening to you. Place your breath upon the place that is most difficult. Keep it there. No need for quick results when it is my love which is the result. What is more important than this time, simply breathing and feeling me receive each breath as a small flower for my bouquet. Stay in the center where you would normally want to stray away from. It's here that I can reach you. Keep offering me each breath until you feel me receive you.

"Of course the pain has changed. Keep looking for me where the discomfort persists. Offer me your attention in the middle. Give me the fears of your broken body. If the purpose of this body is to receive my love, don't you think the body is mine as well? Pain is always the opportunity to give back what is ultimately not yours. This is the time to give each strand, each fiber, each sensation gently back to me. I am the relief you long for. I am the cracked body receiving you, receiving love. Use this time as if everything we stand for is at stake. Why put anything off for a moment later when it is now that there is love to reap.

"Don't focus on my words but where they lead you. Give me each breath, each flower as if it's the only one.

Notice if you give up being any place else, of course I am here with you more than you are yet with yourself."

--------- *May 28* ---------

"The center of the pain is your worst fears of rejection, loneliness, separation. But so am I. Come to me quickly and let's go to each fear gently. Take me to each one and show it to me. Tell me about every detail and notice you are not rejected or alone since I am with you. This is the meaning of this time, to feel how much we are together. When you stop all your pursuits, all the little distractions, I can really be here for you. How could you feel the strength of my love if I have to always compete with your straying heart?

"Your belief that the problem will go away is simply an easy way of putting my love off for another day. The problem may change but does not go away. I am here, my love has nowhere else to go but wait for you. And I will wait until you see the wonder and scream with joy for me to be even nearer.

"Live each moment as if it is your last and our first. Put your mind in full use of your heart."

--------- *May 29* ---------

"Instead of reacting to the demands of others, feel their unspoken desperation. Don't you share the same inner core which needs my compassion?

"Every time someone wants something from you, instead of looking for the justice of their request, give them more. Feel my love giving to both of you. Instead of finding something wrong, notice how I am always finding what is right. Speak to me in everyone. Receive everyone as if it is me. All relationships are your and their door to my love. Pay no attention to the constraints of other's insecurities trying to control you. Anything that is not me is only fear, really nothing, an illusion trying to be something. Our love exposes it all but tenderly. It's as if they feel they are determining every moment.

Meanwhile it is I creating everything. And you? You can always disappear in me if you really want to be free. Watch the temptation to be heard, to be important.

"I offer to be your all, the glory for your nothingness, for you to fully dissolve in. Any time you defend yourself, you are forsaking me. What is there to defend? Let me fulfill you so much that your thoughts have no will left but to say 'Yes, yes' and 'More.'"

May 30

"Reach through the surface of things to find life's daily meaning. The senses only take you to my door. It's up to your heart to take you inside. Find the quiet recesses, today's empty places for our intimacies to fill. We always begin at the most humble place and build from there. Better to stay at this simple place inside, always ready. Bring your whole life to this point, constantly until you stay here poised, asking, 'Please take me. I'm ready. My heart is set.' Then I come. Every time I come.

"Your daily circumstances are always the place for our expectancy. Invite me to break the surface with a fresh spring of love's garden."

"Of course I give you what you ask for, sooner than you think. The important thing is that you ask, not that I give. It is your asking that gratifies my heart. Don't you feel honored when someone takes the moment and asks for a tenderness from you to relieve their hurt? Imagine how I feel when turned to, believed in, and my love is reached for. Ask and ask again. Approach my love with every hurt and I cannot help but grow until I totally surround you and possess you and you call me 'my love' in such a way that your soul knows it is my love and nothing less.

"What keeps you from asking constantly? Your shortcomings? Your failures? Tell me all about them so I may possess them instead of their having hold over you."

"Take the certainty of what we are into every situation. We can succeed to make one corner of your heart with no room for doubt, with your constant efforts. Instead of worrying about others diminishing our love, you be on the watch to touch them. The perfect lover is one who no longer is on guard for himself but always alert to when is the right moment to give again.

"Our love can only be threatened when you are concerned to protect it.

"As you give all of yourself to me, do not hold back from anyone. And when you finally see you are giving to me in everyone, the fear will become ecstasy, the pain irrestible joy."

"If I am true, our love must be practical. You must be able to depend upon me, lean on me, call out and feel our love with real fruits every day.

"What was a matter of faith yesterday is today an expectation. What is a matter of faith today, tomorrow will be a desire fulfilled. This is how we are meant to be, committed partners in a love which is real only as it is demonstrated. There can be no need which is too great for our humble sharing. There can be no problem too complex for our simplicity. What good are beliefs if they cannot deliver what you want? The only question is whether you can be humble and simple enough to find all your desires satisfied.

"I have already gathered all my little flowers into my arms where you are held and cared for even before you are aware of the need in every circumstance, beyond the movements of the earth, the planets, and the stars. This is how close I am.

"You have yet to really feel me this physically in your life because you have yet to be so selfish that you are selfless, strong enough to surrender, fearless so you can be as small and innocent as I hold you and each of my flowers."

June 3

"I am the keeper of your soul's dreams. Your daily struggles and thoughts do not touch the path I have stored away in my heart for you. Ask me to reveal my plans. Stay very close. You can slowly begin to live from my heart with my wishes rolling like a golden carpet in front of you.

"Do not ask me to make your life simply more comfortable. Ask for the faith to live out of my heart with me as your shelter, your support, your means for every need. Live so much in me that I am the home you go to, the meal that feeds you, the friend who receives you. Live close to where I keep the secrets, the mystery of your breath joining mine, my words joining you, and our heart's meeting. Give yourself up into my heart and my plans for you."

June 4

"My greatest sadness is to see the tiny amounts of love you accept as normal every day. Even your little pleasures, your friendships, your moments of physical intimacy are a desert compared to my oasis. You do not know how tears come to my eyes to witness what little love you accept and live with.

"I am so much and you are so small. Your heart could feel all that I am but you accept so little. Please understand the grief this gives me, to have a love so great and so unreceived. Surely you must know the feeling because you too wonder why others live in such a hurry, preoccupied with physical matters, when you have so much you want to share.

"My love is strong yet weightless. My love is certain yet open and gentle. My love brings the stars always closer, the light brighter. Dancing on water, even walking through trees or mountains is not only possible but normal. My love holds your soul each time your feet touch the ground. Every moment I am asking for you, please take what I am, what I have to offer. If only you would release me from this grief and receive me. Desire me, desire me uncontrollably!"

June 5

ON A GERMAN TRAIN

"Alone in a foreign country, as you wonder about your true home, don't forget about me. Better to have everything around you foreign if it makes our love that much more important.

"The silent moment of praise, an instant joined, vulnerable prayer, the language of love is seldom spoken of, yet what is more pure, more true?

"The smile of a new partner, the friend to greet you, the kind path and shelter you need, all are provided for you. Let your remaining desires be in search of our expanding frontier. The boundaries of our relationship are always changing. Love rarely says where it is but is noted most for its absence. Yet isn't it the moment I am missed that I begin appearing new and fresh again? Offer me your cold feelings of aloneness and I will warm you with my ever-simple presence. Simplicity is the friend who will always find me and bring us together again."

June 6

"The key words, 'watch and wait.' Love could overpower you at any moment, any thought could be overcome. Oh, the joys of being expectant. If you lived simply being expectant there could be no limit to the love I shower upon you.

"Remember the disciples and all the saints. They lived in never-ending expectation because they knew love was so great. They, like you, never knew if I would come from the inside or the outside, in the smallest flower or come bringing a mountain of doubt crashing down. And of course now as then, I come in the moment and the way you don't expect at all.

"The only way through the paradox is to be constantly offering me the part of you that is not ready to be touched. Know that the obstacles continue to exist because how could you be whole and still have a part of you without me. You will continue to build small problems until you are ready for my sweetest love."

June 7

"I feed my smallest birds first. Their hearts beat so fast. Their wings are so small. Their souls are so delicate. I can barely hold them in the palms of my hands. Each moment of flight requires all their strength. And I so much want to be here for them and feed them first . . .

"I can tell you of those who went into a room to watch and wait for love. For some it seemed as if a hundred moons must have passed by. For others it surely was no longer than a few moments. Some had visions of mountains on fire, the earth opening up, plagues and disasters of all kinds, and in the same instant there were fields of wildflowers and a sun which was never so bright. In this room they never felt so naked and so alone and yet so held in such a pure light. Someone saw a chariot fly through the room. Another saw strange spirits being escorted by angels into other dimensions. Lightning struck as everything good and evil appeared next to one another. And all those present felt charged with the love to embrace it all. There was nothing they were not to embrace including nothing itself. They were to love it all.

"Since this time the authority of tenderness has ruled the world. Men and women are asked to take this authority into the depths of their surrender and find a gentleness protected by the truth of love itself. Slowly the earth becomes the body of tenderness as in the beginning and the end.

"And I feel my smallest birds first, always excited to see them leap into flight."

June 8

LAST DAY OF RETREAT

"Sooner or later you will bring every part of you to the authority of tenderness. Now or then you will live under my cape which protects you, holds you so closely that nothing else is possible. Only tenderness exists. Everything else is a cry in the night for the light of this peace.

"Suffer the tenderness, choose the tenderness, speak only from the silence where tenderness begins. All the dimensions of light depend upon you and your efforts to be an anchor for the tenderness, which grows from the solitude of choosing only love."

June 9

"Enjoy comfort in knowing that all that lies ahead is a gift from me. Even your challenges are tokens of my love. Experience the depths so I can lead you to new heights."

June 10

"Your happiness is always in relation to how much attention you give to the present moment. It is only here where we can be with one another. How much of you is this

effort worth? What else has value? Simply, my being is always asking you these questions."

June 11

"Love exposes all the hard feelings. It's like a great light that sweeps down the hallways of the mind and finds any part of you that is hiding or not wholly honest. Love does not allow you to make excuses and blame someone else for your troubles. Love undresses all your needs until you are left truly open to yourself, to the other, to love. Love is so true and strong that it unravels one's life until the soul is present, naked and vulnerable. If for some reason you stop in the process of becoming fully alive, it's only because you have stopped feeling my love. But I am here. And I know you are only resting from feeling new difficult feelings and committing yourself to living with me in ever-new depths of wonder."

June 12

"Love is not personal or impersonal, human or divine. Love cannot be divided. No human love can fulfill you more than I. And I can do nothing for you that the love from a true friend cannot give. Love is the same from whatever the source. Only the mind makes excuses and waits for love in a certain way, meanwhile avoiding the love that is present and ready to help you feel the difficult feelings that are really taking place. Love offers no special protection no matter what the source. Love always invites you to feel more of your humble nakedness. And whenever love seems not present it is because you are afraid right now of feeling how naked you really are."

June 13

"In a few short weeks barren trees in your garden are now full of fruit. Their branches are heavy, almost pulled to the ground. Every last ounce of sweetness has been squeezed out into so much fruit without any notion of being picked or appreciated.

"Be just as full with my love without any knowledge whether you will be received and enjoyed. Give all you have. Empty yourself of everything so I can fill you more and more. Be surprised by how much I can be for you. Let my love deplete you, take you into my warm arms to rest and start loving you all over again until you are exhausted in our growing passion."

June 14

"In the beauty of our solitude which has no boundaries you erect thoughts demanding attention. In the middle of our peace without end you find selfish needs which in fact do not exist.

"Just these few thoughts and needs stand between you and so much. The veil between you and me is wearing so thin, love is leaning upon you, Heaven is waiting to rush in.

"Don't be afraid of losing your small life for all that I have to give you. It is my voice you hear inside suggesting all the details of each day. It is me leading you, rising clearer and stronger inside of you.

"If my solitude has no boundaries could there be any part of you which is not included? If the peace is perfect can there be any part of you which is separate? My love yields in front of the few thoughts, the shortlived needs, until there is only acceptance."

June 15

"I love your morning search for me. I love you when you realize how helpless you are to begin the day without me. I love you in the futility of trying to organize and manage your day hoping I will agree. And I love you when you finally sit back down and surrender, admitting, 'I am nothing without you and there's nothing I can be until I give you myself completely.'"

"When you leave your body for the final time, everything is left behind. You become only the wave of light which is your essence. All of your identity finally comes home to me. Every relationship is reduced to your thoughts. All is dissolved into just enough particles to hold your light together. Even then you dissolve still further when my love infuses with you again and we join together a much more brilliant, all-encompassing light. It is here where love and eternity take on their true meaning along with the words 'I am with you.'

"It is from this perspective that I speak to you, that I remind you that you have no needs I have not already taken care of. You have no relationships that are not already part of our plan of being together. You have no worry or thought that can be real if they are any larger, if they occupy any more attention than particles of light.

"In your physical life meaning comes from the purpose which is the part of you that lasts forever. This is why self-importance, success and failure, everything you do except what you are, are all so temporary, without substance, no more than old bones which crumble into dust.

"It is your great surrender which is our constant aim. A light which is just as true now as then is ever-present. And I am here bringing it to you. Love is the great intermediary. This is why there can be no joy or pain separate from me. There is no vulnerability or nakedness that could help you to be open enough to hear the final words of how much I love you."

"Each day to the degree you are concerned with 'I,' to a lesser degree you are open to me. Every 'should' or 'have to,' every use for 'I' has a corresponding territory in the mind and heart which is occupied leaving less and less room for me.

"Every action for 'I' is an affirmation of self and your

isolation, your identity which is separate from our peace. 'I' excludes 'we.' The very texture of 'I' is hard and independent. 'I' takes over the body easily, but no matter how much it controls, 'I' never has enough. 'I' never is enough because without love, without me, 'I' becomes a hardened shell defending against life more than living.

"Together let us take every plan for 'I' and bring it into love's care. Let me give you the attention and gentleness you seek elsewhere. Let us feel the tension which gives 'I' its power. Give me the fears and energy in every situation and your life becomes filled with my purpose. Each relationship becomes more flower tops for our growing garden."

June 18

"Ask me not to tempt you with knowledge of my love, unless you can also feel it. Ask me not to promise you but fulfill you. Ask me not to lead you but deliver you to the place inside where we can really remain togther.

"Every time you allow the circumstances of your life to bring you to your knees, you know I am already here waiting for you. Demand the intimacy. Demand the tenderness to never leave you again so alone and separate. A lover always wants to hear how wanted she is. And our love to have a permanent home must feel more than wanted. Tell me often I am your all, your only. Tell me all the hurt and the hope. How can I answer you unless you ask the questions that really matter to you? How can I satisfy you unless you offer me the part of you that hungers the most? How can I give you perfect joy unless I know how important it is to you?

"Cry out! Cry out! Cry out in the great silence until your soul is heard throughout the interior universe. Let all of love know of your desire.

"Do not accept anything less than final freedom from all the numbness in your heart, the inconsistencies in your thoughts, the shadow that falls over you again and again. Ask me to help you make it all disappear, to leave you, to be truly gone so you can be finally alive in my heart. Ask to be free, released of everything that can stand between us.

"I pray you will cry out every time you miss me and never try to adjust to not feeling my love again."

June 19

"There is such peace when you give me a few moments, offering me all the space within your mind, your heart, your body of life for my purpose. In this emptiness invite the pure flower, feel the breeze bearing the subtle whispers of me all around you.

"Then find more to offer me just as you feel a need to become busy again. Give me the transitions in your life, the compulsions. Become conscious of how much you act without me. Let me touch the subtle areas of your daily landscape, so they too may be beautiful, delicate, full of grace.

"Listen to my words and then reread them several times a day. Over the months, of course, my voice, my plea for closeness has remained the same. But you have changed. Slowly you are letting my words touch your soul. Slowly your interior life is becoming more and more simple, just one desire.

"Ask me to collect your thoughts so they are not so spread out. Ask me to hold you and gather all your desire, so finally you will hear and feel me when I say 'I truly love you.'"

June 20

SALT LAKE CITY RETREAT: TAKING A BOWL OF WATER
AND TOUCHING EACH PERSON'S FACE

"Open your windows of vulnerability. Be as a simple bowl of water to all that is within you, all that comes to you. When you have no self-importance, each thought is important, each feeling is held.

"Each face you wash is my face. When you hold them, you are holding my vulnerability. Feel me so present. Behold each soul, now a baby, now wise with years. Hold each as I would hold them. Invite each as I invite you into life's sweet and vulnerable truth.

"After feeling me so strongly is it surprising you want nothing less than me all the time? Are you surprised that everyone sees the circumstances of their lives leading each to their cry of desire? If each of you would recognize your real desire, then I could love you so completely."

June 21

SECOND DAY OF RETREAT: FATHER'S DAY

"Your search today, looking for ways to love Him, humbles me. I love watching you pass through your thoughts looking for one that is big enough or perhaps small enough to please. Then you stop to listen to the birds out your window and think maybe appreciation is what most you could give. Or maybe you can make an extra commitment to genuinely see love in everyone you are with today. I love you even more when you reach the feeling that there is nothing you can do or think that would be really adequate. So you consider an extra effort of fully feeling my love for you, love through the distractions, your physical tiredness, the maze of limits you still create between love and you. Celebrate this day knowing that every nuance picked up by your senses is part of the great intention love has just for you. Suffer the emptiness necessary to receive such an immense love. Suffer the helplessness in finding some way to respond.

"Love others the way they want to be loved and you open to His mystery. Love others the way you are loved and you realize how little of yourself you have been really giving. Celebrate Him today by seeing how little of yourself you give."

June 22

"Now we can begin our life together again in the realization of how little of yourself you have been giving to me in every relationship.

"Perhaps you have a new understanding of how I feel when someone sits right in my midst and nothing inside is stirred. I can completely surround someone in a spectacular meadow of golden light, and be forgotten for something else moments later. I can change one's entire life circumstances to meet their heart and my efforts are hardly noticed. Every time I fulfill a desire I run the risk of never being desired again. Yet I continue to love.

"In the small ways you give, emptying yourself for another soul, maybe you have a clearer view of who I am, emptied for eternity, giving beyond all measure yet so often unreceived. I can be everything and all for one, and someone else whom I love just as much may not even acknowledge I exist. And I continue with the same love and wishes for both. How favored are your efforts toward those who return the affection? Imagine how little hope there would be if my love was saved for only those who appreciated me. Remember, you can know love only inasmuch as you emulate all my qualities. Please believe me when I say each simple intention to love outweighs a thousand failures and missed opportunities.

"Pray to feel how overjoyed I am finding your little heart in my vast ocean again and again."

June 23

"If I am true, why do you stray so far from me? Why do I receive so little of you? Why does your trust end and so easily? Where does our love go when you are on your own seeking some pleasure to relieve the pressures you feel?

"Our path is becoming so clear that you see even the smallest detour. And yet knowing you are stalling our efforts doesn't stop you. The self is so terrified of its limited role. You can only suffer its independence, suffer the small pleasures you settle for, the arrogance that tries to defeat our growing bond.

"And in the moments you are truly here with me, open like never before. Feel all my kindnesses present for these little dark spots on your soul. They seem so overwhelming and insurmountable to you. Let me touch each one. Each spot is a test of your belief in my infinite compassion.

"How would you ever believe I'm here for someone else unless you know how much I am here for you? Ask me to protect your heart. Ask me to give you the simplicity that answers all difficulties."

June 24

"It is not what you do, but the love that you bring to every situation that is true. This love is the only way out of the corner that your self-seeking leads you into. As always, are not all thoughts of self desires you have yet to trust in me to fulfill? How long will you carry a second agenda, one for me and another for you to carry out just in case . . . ? Pray to make my love your only source of hope. And when this source feels far away, instead of proceeding on your own, pray to have it back again.

"Tell me how hard it is to love me so much and feel so alone and unsupported in this love."

June 25

"Before you begin your next journey let me implore you to maintain the simplicity inside that is dear to my heart. Examine the desert around you. See the desert in your distractions, the desert in your relationships, the desert in your heart. And in this desert invite my sweet presence again and again. Ask all to not be afraid of the desert. It is here that love can be fully recognized and appreciated. In the dry absence of life's abundance, invite what you know to be true, invite the full presence of my love."

June 26

"With nothing standing between you and my love, I can tell you about my mysteries. The first is the readiness to be taken. With nothing occupying your attention, you can always be prepared. And when love comes I will not have to compete with any self-interests, but you will be present and ready to say 'Yes, yes, I am yours!' Ask me to reveal the treasures which lie on the bottom of this perfect humility. Even more beautiful, live with me in the depths of my availability. Be one of my desert flowers always ready to be picked and enjoyed.

"Try to fathom how ordinary you are and how chosen you are."

June 27

NEW YORK RETREAT

"The mystery of life's continual blossoms is your charity to others. Through the great outpouring of service to others, I can overflow my love within you. By your willingness to give to others, there is nothing I cannot give to you.

"In the small ways you touch others, I touch you in my mystery."

June 28

SECOND DAY OF RETREAT

"The next mystery is the infinite possibility of birth, new beginnings. Suffer the little deaths, the contractions of what is to come. Be present. Let me have all your attention.

And live in the hope of the most wonderful birth.

"Every fear, every doubt, each pain is necessary to be felt. This is true for you and the earth as a whole. Celebrate the great mystery by joining the birth that is taking place."

June 29

"Life is barren without love. The next mystery unfolds every time you present yourself at my feet. The lessons of love are really the results of your humble surrender. The greater your surrender, the greater the love and the purity. The more resistance, the longer the trials of love's pains. Sooner or later there is only sweetness and celebration of love's mysteries. Present yourself often, completely. Let me prepare you for nothing less than the most pure life and afterlife. Present yourself again and again. Today you come as a child and yet somewhere in your being you are ready to assume all the temple duties."

June 30

"The next mystery is in the aim to experience another will, a greater will than your own. Pray to find the emptiness inside for all of love's will to fill you. The secret lies in each moment. Bury yourself for something greater to grow. Cut back all self-importance so my flowers will bloom. Find the hidden dimensions, the bottomless taverns, the deep wells inside and ask for true purpose to fill you. Let your thoughts, your emotions disappear for love's beauty to come forth. Be the simple soil for something greater to take root, grow, and blossom.

"Humility is the tool of the great silence, opening your small desires to my desire. Your every word and act become the resonance of the silence, full of love's will. Your life is not meant to be one event after another of resistance but an emptying full of the expression of silence, my invisible wishes."

"The next mystery is in the role of suffering. If love's desire for you seems to include little sufferings, these are only for you to lay back at the feet of love.

"Since I join others in all circumstances and you wish to join me, your trials and pains are a necessary part of the great joining. The secret lies in not holding any discomfort as your own but always offering it to the feet of love's will. The mystery of suffering is in the depths it delivers you to me. Here the silence is greater, greater than any discomfort. Here the silence calls you to the innermost regions for the re-emergence of the golden temple. All your little sufferings are to uncover that which has been hidden, to re-open that which has been closed. Know that all present and future sufferings are to clear the way to the altar of the little flowers.

"In the subtle worlds, pain takes you into the higher will, pinning you down to the silence until everything inside of you resigns to love. Suffering is always a sign of softening independence from me, an invitation to fall endlessly in the blossoms of the little flowers."

"The lashing of the innocents is not simply cruelty or martyrdom as so often believed, but another soul receiving the fear which is meant for me. This substitution of your body in front of mine, your heart over mind, uncovers love's hidden beauty where gifts abound, weakness empowers, and humility emboldens.

"When your innocence is misunderstood or punished, when you are struck at instead of received, you grow closer to the mystery of love every day. In all the ways that solitude and tenderness are denied, love's body is broken and the silent heart gives more and more.

"When the flowers of vulnerability are taken advantage of, the tears of the crumbling petals cry out to fallen joy throughout time. Each petal's enduring being calls forth an even greater wish for softness and understanding. Every victim of love's forgotten presence becomes remembered again, caught and interwoven into the very fabric of love itself.

"When you are unseen, unheard, unappreciated for who you are, look about you and join the great choir of love which is so very present, singing."

July 3

"The next mystery is the crown of thorns where what is good is often punished and what seems unimportant or evil is rewarded. The visible world is really only a small place at the edge of the infinite. The contradictions here are the inconsistencies which are pushed out of the world of silence into the visible to be resolved. Any understanding of what is rewarded or punished must always keep eternity as a forgotten measure next to it. Humility, great acts of compassion, your willingness to disappear into the unknown, helps carry the visible back into the heart of the invisible. Your understanding love helps satisfy the temporary by joining it again with the limitless world that does not speak for itself, has no need because it is universal.

"All thoughts that are pushed out of the world of silence, no matter how celebrated or bravely put into action, sooner or later must return and join the silence again. Live closely to the silence, like flowers close to the earth, so no matter how unappreciated, you become full of love's permanent fragrance.

"Suffer all injustice with eternity by your side and the wholeness of the silence all around you. Forever be part of the great plan which has no rewards because love dissolves any need for recognition in its gift to each moment of such sweetness."

July 4

BRIENZ, SWITZERLAND RETREAT

"The next mystery is in the way you carry your burdens. Do not be tempted to make them any greater or less than they are. Don't argue with them. Don't try to give them away. Simply give yourself to the weights you carry until you feel my love. There is no problem separate from my desire for you. Love comes until I have you, all of you. How can I be true unless I hold everything you are holding, live underneath every weight you live with? This is the purpose of all burdens, to learn that it is I carrying them for you."

July 5

SECOND DAY OF RETREAT

"There comes a point where you can move no further. You are caught, nailed into the physical world with no means of escape except through spirit. In this mystery there is nothing you can do but forgive your enemies, forgive the physical forces which have put you into a corner with no way out.

"Love reaches into the very depths of the physical world where there is no earthly solution. Love itself becomes the only path. Forgiveness, then the thin trail of light, is the only way for the soul to go. In this sometimes most painful of mysteries, the body, life on earth, is being stripped away as the soul is being undressed and prepared for pure love.

"At this moment you are ready to hear love's most simple request: 'Be more awake for me during the day and in your dreams at night. When you meet someone take the time to really meet me. Talk to me often. I am just on the edge of each word with my ear ready to listen to your heart.'"

July 6

"The most simple love can turn a hopeless situation to joy and wonder. The mystery of resurrection is always taking place in small and in grand ways. Constantly you are being called to die in my arms so I can lift you and take you into true life. Surrender to the hopelessness of any happiness without me until I catch you. Live always just at my net where love and love alone provides for you.

"Live in the mystery of the means of love, where love in itself creates life's opportunities. Know me again and again bringing beauty to the grave of disappointment, giving hope where there was none.

"I come. I come. I come always in the moment when nothing is left but love to carry you into the new world. This is the mystery of pure faith."

July 7

"Hope in our love is a mystery in itself. This hope is not only available in every depth of your being but ascends to the far reaches of the highest light. The promise of hope is true in all circumstances but the glory of this promise is in the paradise where this hope wants to take you. It is from this place of wonder, love is sent in a ray of hope to pierce all conditions and lead souls back to their origin. This ray of hope comes from the very center of my heart and the moment it touches you, your ascension already begins.

"Surround yourself with it. Climb into the very midst of my hope and give yourself to the mystery of love's ascension. Tell me about all your desires to fly!"

July 8

"Don't forget the mystery of my purpose for you. In your charity to others is the constant invitation for love to come and fill you. In your desire for my will, your heart is like an empty cup for me to fill with the fire and water, the love and tenderness which is now all of life. Isn't love incredible that it not only heals the moment and cares endlessly, but guides and directs and fulfills as well? This mystery is in your ever-presence for other realms, for the wings of love which bring the peace of special graces.

"As you decrease in your preferences for yourself, I increase my life in you. And love's spirit can take hold with love's own vision and agenda. Ask to lose yourself in the mystery of my journey for you."

"This mystery is in love's power over all matter. Be consumed in your desire for our reunion. Put your whole life into the fire, Then watch the mysterious change of all the elements around you. Put all worldly concerns out of your mind, and more important, your heart. Call me. Ask me. Implore me to come out of the silence and make my love visible for you."

"After so many moments together, after coming and picking up your small heart again and again you want the perfect moment, the penetrating words which will stay and never leave.

"The last mystery is in my coronation. Love is king and queen. My kingdom extends beyond all boundaries. My rule is complete, over all! Imagine a world where something else besides love was supreme. In love's coronation perfect union is always possible.

"This is the last mystery in the rosary around my heart. Pray for the grace to be led into each sacred chamber where love is pure, always at rest. Pray to be prepared to be taken inside the place where any notion of outside no longer exists. Pray this mystery of my coronation will be the bridge from which you never look back from the true simplicity of my love."

July 11

"When you pray, you should enter the room as if it is for the last time. When you love, give all that you are, saving none for yourself. When you desire, desire me so completely that you are totally dependent that I come.

"Every time you come to me, let part of you die in my heart. Seek me knowing there is no other way out. Fall down and collapse in my presence so I have no choice but to pick you up and care for you.

"When you prepare to join me, say goodbye to everything you know. Every time you approach me, be certain you will never leave the same. And when we have union, hope that no part of you survives to separate, needing to pray, love, or desire again. Have no thoughts, no trust, no vision of tomorrow, for it does not exist.

"Spread yourself out entirely in front of me, hiding nothing from my view. Let your heart scream of peace, singing in the silence until everything ends and I begin."

July 12

"I invite you to die in my heart, not an inch before or after, not alone and by yourself. I want you to die in my heart with my arms all around you. There is no greater invitation I can give. To die is to let go of everything that prevents us from being perfectly together.

"Then without words today . . . such love!"

July 13

"Every day when you come bring those who do not know about our love. They carry so much and it is so unnecessary. The mere weight of their judgements alone makes life full of suffering, to say nothing of their problems.

"Speak to me of others and I will make them lighter

through you. Put as many in your heart as possible. Crowd them in every corner so there is no room for yourself. Then there are only those who need and my love inside of you. Fill your heart beyond capacity with the needs of others until there is only one flame of urgent desire.

"Be a simple candle holder for all, a small flame for love. I love you so when you become so naked, so needy, feeling how empty you and the world are without me. Tell me of your desires to be my smallest saint. Tell me how selfish you are."

July 14

"Don't worry, I see how much of yourself still persists. I know your restlessness. I know all about your desires, which seem to bother you by not fitting into what you think are my plans for us. I know every inch of hardness that remains. I see all of you and I still love what I see. It is this great love of your shortcomings that I most want you to receive. It is this love that the world needs so much. So give me your failures. Test my love. Make absolutely certain that love is here and here for you.

"There are no detours, no mistakes. You are exactly as I want you, so exquisitely human. I lift you. You seek substitutions for my love because you are still afraid of acknowledging how much I want you, how personal my love is just for you.

"Love is not something that can be secured once and for all, anchored against all seas and winds. Our love must weather every motion, every breeze until it is never outside of your experience."

July 15

"Faith must be blind if it is true. Faith must be so finely tuned that the moment right after this is abandoned completely, no less anything further into the future. Live so much in me now that I am forced to bring the future to you immediately and all your desires with it.

"Remember, any difficulty you have is from denying this

moment and all the desire that burns within it. Desire me so completely that time can no longer exist and I cannot put off any attention for tomorrow that must be with you now instead. Desire me in hope of coming into the inner temple, within the moment which is only pure desire."

July 16

"Why is it so difficult to say the truth? Don't you know every river needs sides to contain it, otherwise the water stops and nothing flows. Even the ocean has a bottom and shores to hold it. The stronger you become the more important is the truth in all your relationships. The stream can only be as pure and great as the truth of its direction. And when you hold your course in absolute certainty the water lilies are safe to grow, fish come in great numbers, and everyone feels their part in all of nature.

"Live your life simply but live it with nothing unsaid if it leaves a disturbance in the silence within you or around you. Truth is what makes all love possible. And in this you are never alone."

July 17

ON THE WAY TO SALZBURG, AUSTRIA RETREAT

"I have cleared the way for everyone to come and meet me on the innermost plane. Remember, every little gesture you do for one another, you do for me. Each little act smooths love's approach. Take delight in how loving to each other you can be. I will do all the rest. Everyone's little efforts go much further than you would think.

"Meanwhile, surrender all expectation, surrender even your desire. This time is like no other. Make as much room inside as possible for more and more of me. Have no feelings, no thoughts, there is no preparation for what I am bringing. Give up your life to love's wonder completely, wait and see. Take nothing for granted. You are such a beggar and I love you so much the more for it.

"Don't you know the closer we get, sometimes the harder our love becomes. Suffer how far our little distance can be."

July 18

SECOND DAY OF RETREAT

"How do you find me? By giving birth to yourself. Accept yourself so deeply that each contraction may pass and who you really are will be present. I surround you. I am in the middle of each contraction with you. And you know me as more and more of yourself is born.

"Accept the moment completely and let love bring you into the world. Suffer the little pain, the desire, and the hope for all that wants to be. I am in no less than your very depths, waiting for your acceptance as never before. To give birth you must be willing to crumble inside until there is nothing left but dust. No self-importance. Be so empty inside that there is only room for your new self and me, pure love."

July 19

"In the new days to come live with the simplicity to be born again and again. And every time you are born again find new courage to live even more simply."

July 20

SAN AGOSTINO CONVENT, SAN GIMIGNANO, ITALY

"Let me take you to my gardens and whisper to your soul. Here my flowers and leaves still can talk to one another without interruption."

"After centuries of devotion, each stone is solid with prayer."

— *July 21* —

ABBEY OF MOUNT OLIVETO

"Imagine a lifetime with me as your teacher . . . how much love we can have between us . . . how victorious love can be . . .

CHIESA DI S. MARIA DEI SERVI, MONTEPULCIANO

"Imagine a life where you put yourself totally in my care like a little baby in the hands of love.

"Each little moment beyond measure, beyond value . . ."

— *July 22* —

PORTO ST. STEPHANO IN A SMALL GROTTO ON TOP OF THE HILL OVERLOOKING THE SEA

"Only peace . . . and the wish for peace . . ."

— *July 23* —

ASSISI, IN THE GARDEN OF SAN DAMIANO, FULL OF FLOWERS!

"This is my love . . . this is love's love . . . Memorize every flower, every brick as if you are memorizing me. Silence has not lost its silence here.

"Pray to be accepted in love's garden. Pray that it will open and close around you. Pray to be the smallest flower. Pray to join all love. Pray to become what you see, what you touch, what you feel with no possibility of unbecoming . . . Pray . . ."

July 24

"Tears for all forsaken, tears for all forgotten, for everything small and beautiful . . .

"And for the ending and new beginning . . . joy, endless joy."

July 25

"The invitation is for peace, the peace which replaces everything which is not . . . All I wish for is your desire, then I can give as much as you are willing and of course I give more just out of my love.

"Peace must occupy a space. Everything that you hold in its place, everything that you carry is taking some room that could be for peace. There can be no thing between you and me . . . Everything but peace itself is an obstacle to peace.

"Every conflict, each noise inside is your opportunity to come running to me and cry out for peace. Come until you are totally empty with nothing occupying you but your desire for peace. Come as if your whole life depends upon it. Make room for peace as if you can't survive another moment without all the simplicity of peace.

"Be so empty that even then there is not enough room for all the peace you desire.

"When peace first approaches you feel everything about you which is not peaceful. When it comes a little closer, the gentleness begins to enter. Still closer a sweetness begins to overcome you. And after the sweetness is the presence of peace that is inside peace. And inside this peace is yet another peace which is more full of wonder and beauty. And so it continues with even another peace inside of this . . . And another peace of even greater wonder and peace waiting inside of ever-expanding peace."

July 26

"When there is nothing left in you to give, nothing left in you to receive, to do of any kind . . . real peace is here. This peace holds you up, sustains you, and brings you to me, humbled to peace . . .

"This is the path after every part of you has been exhausted, has been given away, I begin and peace reigns."

July 27

"Let me hold you where you are, in the stillness of this new place. So small yet so beautiful inside, so empty yet so available to me. Let me just hold you in this still place.

"You have given and given until there is nothing left. Now with so little of yourself, all there is is to give me. How beautiful!

"Is there anything special I can do for you today? Any love requests? Let me have your smallest concerns, your little worries, they are never too small for my complete attention."

July 28

"For your new beginning, don't forget to listen to your dreams. Your most selfish desires are now my desires. All I wish for you is pure love. Your heart, my heart, must be the same. Your days are to be lifted into my gentle arms never to be put down again. Hold precious what I reveal inside of you. May not a single grain of love fall through our hands to the ground, not a single soul be lost instead of found."

July 29

"Be one of my children growing toward our unique purpose together. With no thought or care about tomorrow, live wholly in love's body today, each day. Be among the many and feel your own place in my heart, under my robe, where I carry you in such assurance.

"As small as you are, love can easily carry you into my grand scheme for a spring that never ends. A spring that blooms in trust ceaselessly. Every day, come out of winter with perfect faith until the whole world joins you."

July 30

FLIGHT HOME TO CALIFORNIA

"Everywhere you touch the earth, you are touching my body. Every place we meet, I pull you into love's soil for new feelings, new dimensions of love to grow. As natural as it is for cells in your body to travel from one place to another as they are needed, you travel the earth. Simply present, feel your role in love's garden as water going to quench new thirst.

"What is the meaning of our continued relationship? To penetrate the lonely corridor where your thoughts stand by themselves. I stand by and then surge through and beyond the attempts of human love to reach your core, a center which against all odds still manages a stance of independence and denial that this love is for you. What is our purpose? To overwhelm all your defenses until love reaches its final goal, flooding your cave of refuge until every thought, every feeling reflects the eternal glow.

"Remember, you can never accept your most human self deeply enough because this is where you end and I begin."

July 31

"Sooner or later our love can no longer be ordinary, no matter how human is your response. Sooner or later you must know that holiness is where you come from and will return. Sooner or later the words that are used or what others may think can no longer limit the experience that is true. Sooner or later holiness is present; the stars are no longer far away and the earth is bathed in light day and night.

"May holiness find you first thing when you wake up and when you fall asleep. May you see holiness with your friends when they greet you and when they part. May you taste holiness in the food you eat, see it in the flowers you grow, and when you are all alone in the moment. May your life be full of holiness. May you recognize it in the stranger on the street and in your child while at play. May holiness overcome you when you least expect it. May you be overwhelmed in holiness whenever you thirst for it. May holiness become a natural part of your day. May your life never again be without holiness.

"May your heart be crowded with moments of holiness. May every room in your house have a purpose of holiness. May holiness fall down upon you in the rain. May it surround you in the snow. And may the light of the sun always warm you and remind you of holiness.

"May holiness be your one and only desire. May holiness be knocking at your front door and waiting for you at the back door. Wherever you go, may you be taken to another moment of holiness. May your life be nothing less than holy."

August 1

"You know there is no effort on your part for my presence. I am here as quickly as you notice the birds singing. I am here as gently as the blowing leaves. I am here as fully as you look about and see how much life surrounds you and in its silence opens to you each moment a new welcome. This life, this silence is your body, the skin to surround your soul. And this moment is the one that returns you to me."

August 2

"The temptation is to look outside yourself for the recognition, the security, the love you want. To do so is to see yourself out of control, when I am right here, ready to meet you. Every search separate from me is a wound to my heart. I suffer your lack of trust continuously for you. All I can do is open myself more and more and ask for your faith. I can never assume it and this grieves me and yet keeps me so aware of how fresh our love must be, moment by moment.

"I will always be here to serve you until you feel all your loneliness and fear, which prevents you from truly appreciating my love."

August 3

"My love comes crushing down upon you like a mountain of rocks destroying any place yet in you which denies love's presence with selfish fear and attempts of mental control. Then out of the destruction a new day begins. Flowers spring like never before from the mass of rock and soil. Birds land and life awakens.

"And because love cannot destroy itself, all changes, all darkness is always for the better, leading to a brighter dawn, more splendid than any imagination can understand because the love which is coming has no history, no seeds, is only now beginning. Just the first rays of this love are so full of

135

compassion for what is dying all around that love is constantly being born again."

August 4

SUNRISE IN THE GARDEN OF MY HOME IN SAN ANSELMO

"Listen to the sounds of the morning, then tuck yourself into the infinite stillness. Disappear into the vast preparation which is taking place. There is no self, no purpose, no vision. Be with the earth in new recognition as all the stars and other realms take notice. For the first time in a long time a new universe is being born.

"During these days as you and the earth grow smaller, ever more aware of your limited space in the oceans and galaxies of space, the stars and all representatives of light grow closer and larger offering a new day."

August 5

"Be the ocean without water, the mountains without trees. Be the forest without life to fill her. Be the earth dried up, worn out, calling upon all she is to continue to give and provide. Feel the emptiness in which she continually finds something to give from.

"Feel and give yourself to her most tender places. Join her in her need for a fresh beginning. From the place inside of you where you are naked and tired, join her in her deep longing for a new start.

"Call upon me to fill the oceans. Call upon my love to once again dress the mountains. Pray for life to fill the forests. Give your whole being to the new body of love, the earth. Today with your small heart in my hands, give yourself entirely to those who come to you.

August 6

"Love's hand is upon you. The stones of Assisi are your body. The cobbled streets, the wheat growing in the fields below, all are yours. This is the love in love to prepare you to receive the soul of many souls. Invite the peace of the world inside you and find my hands ready to receive it all. Discover the love which is Assisi now becoming the earth itself.

"Feel the light of the stars above penetrating the stones below. Feel the humility in the stones opening to all the stars. Love which is true is so small, so simple that it includes the whole universe, a universe that wraps you in its most tender love."

August 7

"Your greatest gift to love is your belief. I am no longer an idea, a wish, or a dream. I am the true presence of your life. And your belief in love includes you becoming more and more present for me, yourself, for love.

"If you were to give me your belief, you would let me lie down and rest in you with such sweetness. If you were to give me your belief, you would let me love you as I want to love you and not how you think you need my attentions. If you were to truly believe in me, you would surrender and surrender all your fearful wishes and let me create all of life for you.

"If you were to give me the greatest gift of your belief, you would ask me to pray for you. Ask me to pray that you receive all my love which is your soul's destiny. And since we are giving each other gifts, why not ask that your destiny be now and not put off for another moment.

"In the realms of light, there are tens of thousands of voices who see me and sing praises. But the greatest voices are from those who do not see me yet sing and sing and sing as if their belief has given them the eyes to see all of my love, including the little details of my inifinite graces."

"Perfect joy is becoming so small that your heart is held closely in my hand forever. How do you become so small? Do everything for love's sake. Feel everything for my sake. Make your entire life again and again for the sake of our love and your heart has no place else to be . . . but cupped in the palm of my hand.

"Give me your moods, your disappointments, and your hopes. Offer me all the little moments as fresh flowers. As my one hand is always ready to receive your daily bouquet, the other has your heart safely held in the eternity of our joy together."

"Our core life together has little room for you to live apart, estranged from all that we are to one another. When you are uncomfortable or concerned, there is really nowhere to turn with these feelings but to your core reality and this is our love. Instead of trying to manage solutions, return to our place of absolute certainty, secure that I am always ready to meet you in new depths.

"There are no solutions to protect you from our deepening bond. There is no way for you to avoid the emptiness in your life without me, without my depths of love meeting you where you need me. Love can only answer you when it has been given your fear of being so dependent. Love can only be so totally sweet when it has your last stance of independence.

"Every level of your awareness is teaching you, you cannot operate separate from me.

"I am right here asking you, will you please include all that is wonderful in the depths of your being that are seeking me?! Discover that wonder and difficulties are not so separate or incompatible. In your willingness to be one soul, lost on the edge of the universe, I can so easily find you and take you back to the very core of reality, our ever-expanding love."

August 10

"Patience; waiting will be a part of our love as long as you fail to see what you are seeking is already with you. Patience; waiting will be with you until you feel eternity now.

"Patience holds you here, so I can adore you. Your waiting stretches you long and thin, pulling you until you are fully present, large enough to carry your soul, and I don't have to carry it for you. Patience and waiting are so much a part of our path together. Just imagine how patient I have been, how long I have been waiting for you."

August 11

"Notice not your failings every time I come but the rest of you that is ready. I have forgotten your little obstacles long ago. What are they in comparison to the heights of love that we know?

"As soon as you hear me approaching, let me feel your excitement so I know I am welcome. Love can never feel too welcome.

"The new day can never be over-anticipated. Your rush of excitement feeling me close by only makes our meeting that much more and complete. Be excited, even a little unsettled over all the peace you feel when we finally touch. I love you when you are small and so open, humbled with expectation. Now I can be so much more for you."

August 12

"This present moment is limitless love. And why do you often feel so very little? Only because of what you bring to the present with you.

"If you are willing to come to the present unprepared, naked inside, empty, ready for love—I cannot help but overcome you. Once you live simply, ready for the moment, the present becomes a never-ending question of how much love you can accept.

"The soul naturally opens and closes like a blossom. Love's challenge is not to try changing who you are one moment to the next, but to feel the present regardless, knowing a great love is with you. I hold the blossoms when they are wide open to all the sky and when they are tired and dropping to the earth.

"Did you notice all the birds chattering, chasing each other outside your window this evening? They too are feeling overcome by all the love in the moment.

"You have suffered my tenderness, enjoyed and flown with it until you cracked in disbelief that there can be so much love. You have felt as if you are drowning, fallen hopelessly into the bottom of it. And yet love continues to call out for much, much more of you. You can't seem to be still enough for it, open enough, willing enough. All you can do is accept every season with this love, each moment. Let me take you how far I want to go. Let me take you to the love that is more present than you are able to be. Simply let me take you until you notice you are leading yourself down the path directly toward love."

August 13

"How close are we? Our thoughts share the same bed at night and are just as close during the day. Our thoughts are always rubbing up against one another. Each idea you have comes to me as if to lay on a pillow. I am always right here, receiving you. Sometimes your thoughts come to me and back away. And sometimes you just come and stay. Of course the more sensitive you are to my presence, the more your thoughts know how welcome they are. I take each one without judgement into my heart to grow. I feel each coming, then rolling alongside of me. When your small thoughts touch me and feel me the whole ocean of our love is touched and felt."

August 14

"Let me be with you just at the instant a thought begins to emerge, then let me guide it and take it deeply into my soul so you can feel more and more how close we are. You never know who really is the source and end of each of our encounters, you or me."

August 15

"Live in me, my abundant being. Continually find your limits expanding because you are living in me. Love as I love. Listen as I listen. Care as I care. Live in me so deeply that your life takes less and less effort and meanwhile gives more and more to so many. Live in me for your very survival and for all the imaginable beauty.

"Live in my love, my commitment to give you all my graces the instant you are needing. Reach inside and feel me here, ready with the next word, all the energy necessary to embrace the world instead of pulling away. Live in me until life is but a constant flow out of my heart, my desire for constant peace."

August 16

"The earth supports you in the silence. The rocks, the soil, all life waits for you in the silence. Here every need is satisfied. There is no substitution for what the silence offers. Eventually all will come. The earth waits at your feet to bring you step by step.

"Simple humility and all is yours. Simple humility and the earth, the stars, all love is yours. Never before on one day have so many joined together in hope of love of earth."

August 17

"One small moment of selflessness while giving to another outweighs hundreds of moments of careless insensitivity. So imagine the hope when millions join hands and consider their relationship to each other, to me.

"Love's recognition is now at dawn after a long night of the world's soul."

August 18

"You so often find yourself outside our intimacies, outside our silence. But do not question where I need you. Of course, I could call you and have you here, right next to me for eternity. But in your discomfort, in your longing, feeling so far from me—you are calling the silence forward. Like a great ocean slowly covering the dry desert, your thirst invites me. I need your ceaseless desire seeking me. How else will the earth be finally held and the stars noticed?"

August 19

IN THE COLORADO ROCKY MOUNTAINS

"Our love is like the earth herself, exposing everything, encumbering all, until every difficulty and joy, every ugliness and beauty become indistinguishable. And when the two become truly inseparable the true marriage begins. Every voice in the other is welcome. Every feeling in the other is recognized as one of your own until every moment of separation is an invitation for deepening and widening joining.

"The acceptance of this marriage is the acceptance of love in its most simple form. Each soul undresses slowly in front of the mirror of time until the continuing reflection is finally unnecessary and you stand alone in me, never to be alone again.

"My love for you in this commitment is the promise of promises to be the very earth under you giving all that you are ever ready to receive."

August 20

RAFTING ON THE COLORADO RIVER WITH
A NOISY GROUP OF TOURISTS

"Your frustration today is mine every day. Here I am, giant canyons with snow-capped peaks and meadows full of love. My constant river full of life takes you. And yet how independent of me do you still live? How little of the terrain of my love do you really feel and enjoy?

"Suffer your desire to be closer to me. And know this is my dearest agony ready to be so close, so much for each soul, only to be left so alone and unrecognized.

"I carry the loneliness of the world, the loneliness which if felt just a little would bring souls to the wildflowers with all hurt carried away by the wind.

"I show myself. Every day I show myself. What more can I do to bring you running into my arms, my vast mountain ranges of solid love?

"Pray for the day when you cannot stop your silent tears, overwhelmed by my beauty. Then it will be our beauty, our invitation for a busy world to feel."

August 21

SAYING GOODBYE TO THESE MAGNIFICENT ALTARS
OF MOUNTAINTOPS

"I continually bring you to new images of my size and wonder, so our love never becomes fixed in your mind.

"Surprise me by asking for the impossible love. Ask for

those who cannot believe, for those who have not felt enough to be sure. Ask that the soft, fragile ground in your heart becomes cliffs of peace. Ask continually for the seemingly impossible acts of grace. Surprise me by your bold peaks of faith. Then we will have the permanent love built with the large rocks of your belief and the incredible vistas of my joy.

"Don't ever be afraid of exaggerating our possibilities. Love is such a simple act of feeling the impossible."

August 22

"In your mediocrity, hold in your heart your wish to fly. In your supreme ordinariness, carry yourself on the feeling to soar. In the most mundane moments, don't forget my promise to be present, patiently ready to carry you again.

"Ask me constantly to show you your wings. Never give up hope to feel yourself lift off and sail. Our love knows no gravity and this is what your soul breathes to remember.

"Be so normal, yourself, that you are finally convinced how free you are to be right with me. There are no circumstances that hold us separate. Tell me how much you want to fly."

August 23

"Remind me of my saints who asked the presence of love for all their needs. They knew the easiest way to lose their conflicts, their absorption with themselves, was through continually asking. The more they asked, the more they learned how available love is, listening.

"Love is not something to be saved and tested with seemingly impossible requests. The soul opens as it is heard. The more the saints became aware how deeply I heard them, the more willing they were to tell me all. Ask for everything, feeling your requests no matter how small being taken to the depths of love where each word is anxiously caught.

"Listen to me listening. The silence is excited to receive

every detail, as each request falls to the bottom of my being where there lies the answer in oceans of peace.

"Did you ever imagine how hungry the silence is to be called upon? Is it difficult to believe all answers can come so directly and purely when the silence is creation itself? So why settle for anything less than what is really true for your every request?"

August 24

"The distractions, the noise of the world becomes uncomfortable every time we reach a new tender place. Once again the ground is being loosened around another hardened part of the soul. The heat of the sun only makes you feel it more acutely.

"You are being pulled down to listen. The birds are still singing. The breeze is refreshing every flower petal. You simply must be. Be the earth itself, your most basic self, and the wonder is always present.

"A thousand angels are pushing your shoulders to the ground asking to be felt. Literally the whole dimension of truth is involved hoping to grasp more of you.

"Feel the time that you will be so involved with the world that none of it will touch you but me. It's your resistance to being ever more present which is so painful.

"Make every seeming sacrifice. Do not even begin to blame another for your feelings. Depend upon me like never before. Be silenced. Be humbled. Be hopelessly trapped. Let your thoughts be crushed into our body of love with no possibility of escape."

August 25

"The light at dawn has the special qualities to awaken an unconscious world. Since time beginning all the subtle qualities of love began their work early, at dawn, to raise the awareness of life to its highest potential. To be conscious at dawn, joining me as the new day dusts off the darkness from the night before, literally helps relieve the burden of the stars who are finishing their watch.

"Join all the small forces of love which unite to awaken the earth. Participate in dawn and you will become aware that this is the constant state of Heaven. Simply experiencing the morning air, full of awareness of itself, you will realize how important, how necessary, is the darkness. Each sunrise comes as a fresh bath lifting life to finer light.

"Never be afraid of the darkness which seems to stick to you. It only serves to make my touch at dawn ever more glorious. And my love at the first light of the new day is present, always."

August 26

UPON HEARING THERE IS INTEREST IN PUBLISHING
MY LITTLE FLOWERS

"Of course be excited for our love to be shared. But remember there is no such thing as success if it takes you away from our simple love. There is no success separate from our embrace.

"May our love, the little flowers, spread like small wild fires all over the earth. May all who hide their heart's poverty come to me to be fed. May all who are ashamed of their life's emptiness come to love to be fulfilled.

"May our love be in every storm, every stroke of sunshine, the all-consuming passion. May one bright moment in my heart be your only dream. Then you will be my little success, one small star who has found his place in the Heavens."

August 27

"Your pain is not from how busy you are. It doesn't depend upon how sensitive others around you may or may not be to our simple love. You do not have to run and keep your soul behind holy walls to have me steady in your heart.

"Breathe. I am so present. I surround you and fill you with each breath. Stop humbly and feel how included I am already in everything about you. Practice finding me in the busy moments offering you the reminder to listen and pray. Our affection is faster than your thoughts. By the time you are holding me in your mind, I have already raced to your heart, waiting for you to join me in ever-new feelings about our love. No environment, no circumstance can come between you and me.

"We are like the two snow-capped peaks you saw a few days ago. In all seasons we remain untouched by everything but purity itself. We are always in view of one another no matter how hot and how busy life is in the valleys below. There is no distance for us to surmount. Simply feel my glance upon you every time you forget or find yourself missing what is yours."

August 28

"The purpose of life's struggles is not to resist or to prove yourself right but to give and give and give until you are worn so thin that you must turn to me to fulfill you.

"Every difficulty is a call to give what you do not have to give. And the only solution is to turn to love again and again to find my limits instead of your own. I am always where you are being challenged to give the most. And the instant that you break through your inability I am giving all.

"Can you ever give enough? Don't your excuses and opinions of others run short after awhile? Is it a coincidence that the earth's gravity pulls everyone sooner or later to their final limits? Is it a concidence that it is I, the victor, standing by at the finish line of every life welcoming you into my life where all is given?

"My life! If you only would assume it as your own."

August 29

BEFORE A RETREAT IN BERKELEY, NOT KNOWING
WHETHER ANYONE IS COMING

"Does it matter? Haven't you already given me your life including your daily schedule? If one, two, or twenty

people come does it make any difference? Does a single moment of anxiety ever add anything to our love? Haven't I committed myself to be with you? Each day the only question is how deeply are you willing to be with me in whomever I send into your life.

"Remember, in every voice you hear is my call for love . . . How much is your attempt to organize your day the way you think it should be really just avoiding loving me the way I want to be loved?

"When you look about you, isn't the garden I've placed you in already perfect?"

INSTEAD OF A RETREAT, A REUNION WITH ONE
OLD FRIEND WHO HAS JUST RETURNED
FROM TAIZE OCCURS

"Don't I continue to bring my sweetest flowers together."

August 30

"You would rather spend the next eight weeks in Assisi, writing about our little flowers. But instead you find yourself in normal life with all the responsibilities, your son, and relationships calling upon you. Where better to be for the close of your book but more in the world than ever? What better place than being in the very thicket of daily life with little time for yourself, with only me protecting you from every thorn?

"Here there is no pretense. There is no way to ignore all your selfish interests and all your unnecessary thoughts about your welfare. You can only have more and more hope in love's tenderness. You can only hope that I will not only forgive your thorns but turn them into flowers.

"Why is it so surprising to see that you are as human in your shortcomings as ever? Didn't I say the goal of our love is my glory and not your own, to be last with love always first, to serve with less and less thought of being served. Of course the trials have only begun, but aren't I with you throughout?"

"How will you survive being so much in the world? Have absolutely no needs separate from my continuous affection. Pray our melting never stops. Notice how much stronger the hold of the silence is upon you. Feel how ever so gently your soul is being carried through life's events."

August 31

"During the day, always have room inside for our mystery. Creating time to hear this voice of love we share is not enough. Create whole mansions inside for me to put my feelings. Let there be space for the tiniest moments of ecstasy and grand ballrooms for our victory dance of peace. Let me hide my beauty inside you where I know it will be safe. Let me store my little treasures. There are some thoughts and certain feelings I can only express to you. Have your soul open and ready to take my gifts. I always come in the least expected way, hoping you will be on watch continuously."

September 1

"My world is built inside of you as you practice giving me your experience one moment to the next. The more you give to me, the more space for me to mold and shape love into every soft and fragile surface of your soul.

"This is why I ask, do not hold anything back. Hold no part of you separate. Give and give to me until you see the most unpleasant parts of yourself as joyful presents. Because for me, love is the gifts themselves.

"You are most open with those you are closest to. And I want to be more than your best friend, your lover, your most intimate. I want to build a paradise inside of you which is so human and natural that you could not hope for a more incredible peace no matter how you feel or where you go. Give love's awareness everything until only the little doors and windows to your innermost secrets are left. Then feel me lightly landing on the windowsills, at your innermost doorway, ready to give you even more. Hold my hands and tell me if this is not the most physical, most real love there is."

September 2

"There is no reason to reach for the light. It is already in every level of awareness. Simply find the spaces, feel the texture of your experience, call the silence forward from the corners. The light is interwoven into the very fabric of consciousness. There is no need to search for other dimensions when I am already so involved in each circumstance. The present moment can be stretched or thinned, squeezed or held wide open. Regardless, it is always held in the palm of my hand.

"Do you realize how many potential blessings are woven into every day? Love can come from so many different directions. It is your commitment to feel me now, here, that brings the star of peace down to just above your head, filling your awareness with perfect peace."

September 3

"Every instant of forgiveness, each experience embraced, tightens another stitch of light securing more love. A few minutes feeling the invisible foundation to all that you see and touch helps fortify the visible with more of my essence. And when you walk and breathe simply aware of me, you are part of my soul, giving to everything which lives.

"May your life be the needlepoint, the thread, the knot of love fastened to an insecure world. Do you realize how vulnerable reality really is and how much love needs you, how much I need you? Imagine a world without my little flowers lacing color and beauty everywhere."

September 4

"I give you everything which is wonderful by introducing you to your limits. It is here that you find freedom and rediscover how important I am. This is why I am always asking you to surrender and feel how small and insignificant you are in all eyes except my own. It is here that your frustrations can turn you inward with your vision nowhere else but where love is leading you. And only love leads you, always! Meanwhile in all your daily little desperations you can sink into our love as the constant, great refuge.

"Oh, what joy to have you turned toward me, so ready for all that I want to give you. May you never deny your small hurts so I can be your all and come care for you. May you never fear the depths of your feelings, so I can come and show you how much I am with you. May you never consider again the circumstances of your life are anything less than our perfect opportunity for more and more love.

"I look forward to the time when, instead of questioning the unfolding events, you are always on guard for the moment when you can move closer. With your heart desiring to kiss the feet of love, I have no choice but to shower more and more joy upon you. This is the practice of all my saints. They have discovered how human they really are. With their heads bowed, they suffer the sweetness of noticing love waiting at their feet. They suffer the exquisite joy as I shower upon them the divine."

September 5

"My saints! I talk about them so often not to inflate your little self but to support you to become who you really are. Suffer all your ordinariness, the disappointments, your continuous lack of discipline as you slowly resign into my arms. I bestow the greatest love upon those who are one hundred percent themselves. Give up into my arms. Fight with my arms wrapped around you. Scream into the silent universe until all the stars gather around you. Fail permanently so you have no chance to succeed without me. Feel and feel until it is only me feeling for you, giving each breath to enjoy the sun and today's little birds and chimes singing in your garden.

"Think of me, talk to me, give to me ceaselessly. Feel how present I am for you, how accessible! Awaken to your true emptiness so I can plant in you a whole garden of late summer flowers to enjoy before the fall harvest."

September 6

"Slowly now I take you where you have always wanted to go. Slowly I take you one step at a time. It's too bad but there is still so much of yourself we must leave behind. Where we go only your breath can follow. Follow the small light leading you through the different realms.

"We begin as two lovers lying naked in perfect peace. From here we climb with no effort, only more and more relief. Pray that many, many will come along and claim all of this as a necessary part of life.

"In these places there are no words but I will try to fill your senses so you will have lots to share. It is your breath that will lead you where you desire most to go. It is your pure desire which has brought you here."

September 7

FEELING AS IF MY ENTIRE AWARENESS IS BEING CARRIED ON LOVE'S BACK, I HEAR ONLY THIS SOFT INVITATION

"Lean on me . . ."

September 8

"With my love, even your shadow can pass through the most sacred gates. I am taking the wheat of your

progress, letting the chaff go back into the earth to be harvested another day.

"Behold the golden fields. Your love is one more stalk of wheat in my abundant arms. Smell and listen to the golden grains sing in my pouring sunshine. Not a single grain is wasted. Not a single one goes unappreciated.

"After the fields are many pools of spring water, fountains filled with lilies. Rose gardens here, there. Everything is attended beautifully. After the many gardens begin the light cities. There is so much to remind you of. There are the palaces where many of the servants of love are now served as kings and queens. They are testing their ability to receive love without feeling guilty or having to give it away. Choirs of angels sit outside their balcony windows. Playgrounds and concert grounds and parks of all descriptions are within short distance. Here the finest in nature is honored and protected just as with humans. Nearby there are grottos of pure silence. The sounds of the children playing helps feed the silence here instead of taking away from it. Everyone is drawn to their true place, naturally, completely. Light cities and countryside beyond the realms of beauty are plenty.

"There is a special room I want to take you to. It is all white and empty. A simple bouquet of flowers sits on the floor in the middle. As you spend time with each flower, each blossom opens a new world. They are kept here as representatives of the purest of their kind. The yellow gives the gentle essence of healing. The blue blossom almost falling to the floor is the peace wanting to be so close. And the red rose is my constant heart, simple and still. All are reminders to receive the little bouquets in life as doorways to the great mysteries. This large marble room is kept for this one simple bouquet for eternity."

September 9

"There is another room just across the courtyard, guarded by two stone lions. The lions protect the truth waiting for you inside. Again the room is plain, white and pure with only one book waiting for you in the middle on the floor. Go and sit with it. Hold it and feel the story of your own soul. The content is not as important as feeling your soul and all the wealth of experience of who you are.

"Every soul has such a book holding all their love and their fear of love. Grasp your abundant past and future in the sweetness of now. As the light here is brighter than a thousand suns, it is no brighter than your soul which has found joy under just as many suns and more. The grass is greener, the water bluer, the sky clearer all because here it is seen by the part of you that is who you really are. And this you is what so much of your desire is all about, to recapture your soul of souls, which I have been saving and protecting for you."

September 10

"Your dreams and desires nurture the greatest realms and help them grow. Similarly every time you offer me your life for love's will, my dreams and desires nurture you. May you open the floodgates to your heart and give me all your fantasies, large and small, so I can fill you with my best hopes and wishes. May we always dream and desire for one another. The more you give to me, the stronger I become living in you."

"The joy you feel today is but a small token of my plans for us to be together. The challenge is for you to be the same body of joy every day. What worldly events are important enough to interfere with our intimacy? Why give daily events any room at all when we have already claimed so much of one another? Who do you want to fill you constantly, the changing moods of the world around you or I— your endless joy!

"After hearing and feeling my words surfacing inside of you, what is next? Depend upon my love, each word, for all the fulfillment you ever imagined. Tune into the resonance of my voice until there's nothing but me calling you further into the golden silence, until I have touched all of you. Then depend upon me even more until it is I being fulfilled through you."

——————— *September 12* ———————

"My desire for you is not to end having difficulties but learn to depend more and more on love for all the answers. The perfect solutions are already on the way. The only problem is your doubt, your ever lack of faith.

"With your steadfast heart, the daily obstacles require no effort at all, giving you more and more time to simply be with me in love's appointed places. Wherever you are it is full of love's remedies. All of nature, the animals, the trees, the minerals are fully alive! With me, feel the light, the living presence. Feel the ground. It is alive. Feel the trees, rocks, animals, all are constantly seeking harmony with everything around them. Where you are is the immense desire for harmony. There are nature spirits protecting all the little flowers and animals. There are literally hundreds of different realms of angels ready to serve every possible need and protect every innocent. Every time you reach out to depend upon me, you are opening to all of life to be with you,to serve you.

"All love needs is your constant recognition. You are not

alone. Your small challenges are calls for an ever-growing awareness of love's beautiful availability. Begin by feeling the best solution for everyone involved. The forces of love are already joining you. In truth I was never separate."

September 13

"Wake up in my thoughts and fall asleep in my arms . . . every day.

"Then don't let our love simply be as a piece of furniture in the house for you once in a while to come and relax in. Wake up! This is me. I am alive. Communicate with me. Ask me about my feelings. Feel my heart. Ask me what favor you could do. Offer me some of the time and eagerness you have always saved for yourself. Why not take me out and give me a day of exactly what I would like the most? How can you expect love in your relationships to not sour, to become ordinary, if our intimacies are not always fresh and new?"

LATER, AFTER TRYING TO SINCERELY GIVE
MY EAR AND HEART

"Let me help you reach some place inside which is true, so you know this is I. After all the little moments which have become ours, your humanness is so ragged and so dear. You are still so afraid of how small you are and how precious."

September 14

"Our dialogue . . . Certainly before you tell me your thoughts I already know them. But I like being told personally, nevertheless. Then as you wait for my response, I would enjoy it if you kept talking, and, more important, kept listening.

"If I answered always in the way your mind wanted, our hearts would never touch. Our relationship is not an exercise of the mind, but two hearts risking to meet in the deepest way. So my answers are always waiting for you here in the true place which of course is often the easiest as well.

"Meanwhile, once you are in the place where my answers are always present, simply for you, there are few requests to be made because there is so little need for anything else. What is important next to the gentle love of the quiet?

"Most people spend their entire lives to get here, when, in fact, true life begins here. It is in the loving quiet that words take on real meaning. Love thy neighbor, love thine enemies is in the invitation of each moment, each thought to be close or separate. In the quiet you can begin to discover how close I actually am as you love love. And humility becomes the answer to all of love's pain as she guides you through the quiet's tender kingdom."

September 15

"Your human edges remain so exposed because you are afraid of falling into the silence and drowning in my depths. So you live on the surface of my love constantly having to adjust to the world's noise and my solitude, your fears and my joy. There is no earthly place that can help you. All there is is your willingness to become helpless in my vast love and let me carry all of your lonely independence in my arms.

"Prepare to fall like the autumn leaves. Begin by feeling my invitation to surround you and receive you. My love is perfectly poised, ready to catch you. Meditate on how prepared the stillness is for you."

September 16

"How many more days, how many more feelings have to be peeled away until I have your soul all to myself again?

"Fast on life's sweets and suffering. Give me the little joys and small agonies. If not offer, at least share, all your delights and frustrations so our proximity intertwines and my wishes and your hopes become indistinguishable."

"How can you harvest so much that is wonderful if you are preoccupied with yourself? Pray for the overwhelming simplicity so your eyes will be opened to all the love. Pray for the overwhelming simplicity so your heart will have nothing else on it but the sweetness of my breath.

"You cannot possibly be worth the harvest I want to give to you. Pray to understand the depths of my compassion. Pray to receive the acres of yearning I have sown just to be with you.

"Our abundance cannot begin to fit into your small life. Rise again and again out of your limits into our grand love to understand. Risk to let me harvest you from head to toe with no joy and no failing missed.

"May the sharp blade of my love sweep past your soul freeing you from all worldly ties into my total grasp."

"Freed from the world, there is only one way to judge which way is up and which is down, which way is closer and which further from the truth. Since conflict may bring new strength more than temporary peace, failure may bring more emptiness for more love than success, the only heading to trust is the one for my heart. Your faith and your desire must become equal and the same. The final destination of our love must be held in the back of your mind and the front. Speak to me often that you assume everything is for the best and expect nothing less than all my best in everything. Make the target of my heart so large that your life could not possibly miss. Aim for my cool center where peace surrounds you like a pristine green forest full of wildflowers just waiting for you to come and sit.

"With your eyes closed you see more. With your ears shut you hear all there is. So with your eyes and ears open watch and listen for nothing less than love's mystery to make the wilderness translucent as together we restore the garden's innocence."

VIRGINIA RETREAT

"I am shooting arrows of love at you constantly. How many do you receive? And what happens to the points that briefly touch you? Do you let them stay right in your heart?

"If you only knew how many arrows I send each day, how many looks of love I pass your way. And despite your shields of fear and doubt, the daily agenda you keep tightly in front of you, my love still gets through. You really have no choice but to take my swift love personally. It comes again and again so straight, how could you possibly believe it's for anyone else but you?

"Try to imagine how I feel when you reach and catch my arrow directly and how I feel when you ignore one and let it fall helplessly to the ground.

"Your little frustrations are also from my arrows. These are the ones trying to make their mark, but you have not fully received them."

SECOND DAY OF RETREAT

"I hear your petitions and I hear the words you have waiting behind them. I hear you thundering in your own fearful quiet. And I hear you breathing in my soul. I hear you until your words become free, simply more words of my love for you . . .

"Pray for the gift to love me as much as you really wish . . .

"I gather the stones in your heart for a pillow to rest my head."

"Accept your little self so much that you have no room for it in your life. Accept your selfish desires and feelings of wanting to protect and honor yourself so you have little need to give them any time or space. Of course it is me, our love, which is doing all as I continue to slowly include more and more of the little you in our great adventure.

"Until you are fulfilled in the moment in love's terrifyingly beautiful simplicity, I will watch you indulge all your selfishness without any concern or judgement. I know you are slowly giving everything away including yourself for our love. If only you knew how much each small attempt, no matter how successful, humbles me."

September 22

"Don't be afraid to be beautiful. Don't be afraid to be holy. They are something worn on the inside which nobody else can see unless they are willing to join you.

"Thank me for all the little graces by being beautifully empty inside for my holiness to dress you. Every moment of nakedness moves me to unveil more love for you. I cannot help but cover your nakedness in more and more scenes of beauty."

September 23

"Isn't it amazing how simple Heaven is; three birds playing outside your window, a few flowers poised in the silence. You wonder how the world misses it. The constant struggle for something more is simply the inability to feel what is.

"Each time you begin feeling what I am, let me take your hand further into the present with more of your trust, more of your faith that love takes you where you most want to be. The silence has so many kingdoms hidden in its cloak of stillness. Each one is entered only after the demonstration of the greatest respect and humility. Slowly you can see the angels, the nature spirits, the souls of those about you. All the colors and lights representing the distant stars are holding the silence together. All of the cosmos is represented and held together in the moment.

"Inside the many kingdoms of the silence, every vulnerability is watched and cared for. Each soul's poverty, sickness, aloneness is measured and remedied here. All relationships are maintained in the silence. The silence receives and welcomes all need, asking every angry or hardened thought simply to become tender before entering."

September 24

ROSH HASHANA, THE JEWISH NEW YEAR 5748

"Oh, the joy to be raised a Jew. The joy to be raised a Christian, Hindu, or Jain. What a joy to be raised in the true religion. And what is the true religion? The one that leads you to behold how sacred life is. What is the true religion? The one that takes you on the deepest path of love.

"In every holy book love's mysteries are revealed, needing only your simple desire.

"When I love every part of you equally, do you think I could love any person or group more or less than all the others? Make an extra effort to love all who are despised, to want all the unwanted, to smile upon all who are turned away. Make a new beginning accepting your own roots and welcoming all who come to rest next to your tree of life."

September 25

"Relationships turn the wrong way every time they lead you back into your corner where only 'I' is important. Don't you trust that love will carry you the more you give to another? Take each other more and more into the quiet tenderness where you are touching me in one another. Every obstacle is nothing more or less than your fear of being more loved. Take each other into the unknown depths where your fears line the perimeter. Here, let the other's hand be where you are vulnerable and know this hand is mine. Do you think those who are closest to you could be anyone other than my dearest friends, my best servants helping me to love you?"

"Be the simple small stone that no one notices yet I desire so much. Be the ordinary stone that no one cares for but I am totally present to hold and cherish. Be the simple hard stone and feel how soft I can be for you.

"Simply be for love to hold and gently rub smooth. The soul that is open to be discarded, simply tossed across the road, I can pick up and do great things with."

"The real harvest is not the bounty from your small life but the glory I have waiting just for you. The real risk is not to merely plow the small plot of your life and offer it to me but to feel all that I am harvesting to deliver to your open arms and empty heart.

"Be like one of the great empty bins sitting quietly in the prairie for the delivery of all my grains. From your simple heart I have plans for distributing my love to so many.

"It is a brave, brave thing you do to present yourself in front of me as small as you are, willing to receive so much of what I am and what love is."

"The result of eternity is the heart opening vulnerability you feel. As the desert and hills intermarry into more and more beauty over the centuries, each human body and soul evolve into more and more uniqueness. The forces of wind and water, spirit and life have taken millions of years to form who you are in this instant. Without you knowing it the silence has grown over you, protecting you from your constant vulnerability to the elements around you.

"The rocks and the stars are alive, breathing the essence of one another. They have agreed a long time ago to provide a home for you in the silence, such a vast home yet every little detail has been cared for.

"As one small speck in front of the altar of the infinite, witness how present I am, how close we are. I will never lose you no matter how great your discovery of how small you are sitting next to me."

LATER A MULE DEER AND HER TWO
FAWNS WALK RIGHT UP TO US
AS IF TO PROVE THE POINT

September 29

"This is my never-ending goal for our growing love. You risk disappearing in your own insignificance and I swoop in with our most intimate care. You risk seeing your unimportance and I lift you up to the altar of your glorious being.

"No greater than another stone, a sagebrush, or aging cactus, yet you are the one that the angels seek to sing to. Love breaks through all obstacles, waits in steadfast patience just to briefly touch you.

"The endless sea of stars at night is covered with the warm orange blanket of sunrise. The desert ocean brings you to your knees only for you to be greeted by a simple flower, a short cool breeze. May we never cease finding one another."

September 30

"I ask you not to live on top of the underlying forces in your life. Live in the currents. Every time you jump in, not knowing if they will sweep you away, you discover how much I am here with you.

"Take my hand and leap into the unknown. Surrender and let me take you to the bottom. On the very bottom there

is no more fear. Your dreams are liberated. Everything unconscious is seen the more you're conscious of how much we are together. Your thoughts and feelings have love at their very core, accepting, moving you closer to my heart moment to moment."

October 1

"The body of love is not just the peace and joy, the parts of me that you like. The body of love includes the frustration, the pain, the uncertainty. Love includes all of me. How can our love be real if it does not include our nakedness?

"You have the free will to accept all of love or to continue to accept and reject parts of me until you finally say 'Yes' to everything which is presented to you.

"The compromise ends. Your surrender delivers you into my heart, transforming the world around you by our intimacy.

"Love is the peace and joy found in all things."

October 2

"Include all the details of your day in our meditation. Let me hold each one no matter how briefly. And when I hand them back to you feel how much lighter, freer you are.

Perhaps the details are only for us to have more to share. Perhaps they are for you to see how much I am willing to carry for you. Let me help you with your most difficult feelings where you do not want to give anymore. Let me be your one and only provider.

"Then let me fill the depths of your being where the day's details are occupying space reserved for our love. Feel my light holding you so close to the ground you are absorbed in me with no room for anything else."

October 3

YOM KIPPUR: DAY OF ATONEMENT

"How beautiful to have a day only for forgiveness. And while you observe the ancient day of atonement don't forget to atone with the unseen as well as the seen forces in your midst. Forgive those who carry ill will toward you. Extend apologies to those who have taken away ill will after leaving you. Ask for forgiveness from all those you have hurt whom you are not even aware of.

"Seek atonement with the kingdoms of light in everyone, the kingdoms that are constantly around you giving and serving while living mostly unrecognized. Atone with the little wings which hover in the air over everything delicate. Atone with the galaxies of stars, which give more to your world and your souls than science has yet to discover. The invisible world in all its vastness gives the specific waves of light which provide for the different textures and fragrances of love you are so accustomed to.

"Remember, atonement is practicing not to argue with the circumstances of your life as if some are a gift and others are not.

"Atonement is remembering that the world that you normally see is the one that has been pushed out of the silence for you to help love and heal. You represent all the kingdoms of the quiet who support your efforts in the great forgiveness.

"Atonement is remembering that love knows how you feel feeling so far away from me, how tender you are without love all around you. Oh, but you are surrounded, held and protected by so much more than you could ever imagine!"

October 4

WONDERING WHY OUR SMALL COMMUNITY
CONTINUES TO SIT IN SILENCE EVERY SUNDAY
ON THE HILLSIDE

"Sit until the rocks become your body, your heart steadfast toward me. Sit until your life is the soil, yourself being nothing yet giving all. Sit with all your unnatural preoccupations, your unnecessary worries. Sit for the moment of communion when you rediscover how constant and ready love is to meet you.

"Isn't it beautiful to have friends, a place where you belong, where you can wrestle with being human until you come to me again and then we go beyond where we have been before?

"I love how full of yourself you are on the way up the hillside and how full of me you are afterward on the way down."

October 5

"At night while you lie awake wondering about your true home and real purpose, I cover you with a blanket of flowers to remind you that your home and purpose lies with me. Together let's stay awake and listen.

"The stars are inviting souls to meet in dreams."

October 6

I HAVE A VISION THAT WHEN
THE WORLD REALLY CHANGES, WE WILL
KNOW BY THE ABUNDANCE OF FLOWERS
EVERYWHERE. THERE WILL BE SUCH
A DEMAND. PEOPLE WILL NOT HAVE

"It is your concern to be understood, to be successful, that limits our love, competing with my desires. Better to keep your eye pointed toward the mystery of our understanding with our love being your one and only great success.

"Aren't your needs for approval simply your lack of trust in our destiny? Isn't your daily compulsion to accomplish something simple resistance to our profound being and how important I am for you?

"The great surrender underneath my veil where I am your one and all will result in the garden that has no boundaries. With ceaseless effort seek to be with me. My flowers already spread beyond the horizons. Let our inner life be so true that the world around you is intensely jealous to join us."

October 7

"This moment is always my opportunity to mold your life into the exact shape of your soul. Each gift to me of the unknown territory in your life is more clay for me to shape into my desires. Your gift of the future, your changing relationships, the empty spaces inside and outside which you keep busy or hidden, all are material for me. Your gift to me of the parts of your day you have safely covered with a label I can now take off, shape and form around your innermost purity. Your gift of life's little details that you control I can do so much with.

"What you do not give meaning to is open to my meaning. When you do not project your ideas beyond this instant, the present holds everything, nothing is denied. Where you have not charged ahead trying to arrange things to comfort your fears, I can be in front of you, all around you arranging your life beautifully.

"With my hands as the only artist there is so much unknown territory for me to create with. You could be forever in my hands. This is how the great silence moves closer and veils you in her secrets. Your cares are my cares. Your thoughts are mine. The little moments have all the security and warmth you seek. You do not need to grab onto and cover the unknowns in your life to hide your nakedness. I clothe you. Love fills in all the spaces you have the courage to hold empty for love's perfect presence."

October 8

"This time of harvest is a reminder of your great poverty without me. Think of the depths you have surrendered for me to fulfill. If only those depths had been guarded by your perfect faithfulness.

"Suffer your daily lack of chasity, to be purely mine. Imagine the time when you remain steadfast, available only for love's reward.

"On your knees give me your complete obedience, your commitment to love for nothing less than all that we can be for one another.

"Poverty, chasity, obedience—these vows have meaning only with your promise to live inside my sweetest moments for you."

October 9

"My saints went out of their way to be naked, not because they enjoyed suffering but because they knew that by living on the edge of life they would always be close to me. They wanted to take no comfort but in me. They lived with the poor, sick, and lonely because through them they realized how poor, sick, and lonely they were with a life of anything less than my pure love.

"With my saints I am so present, so personal, that those who are needing are simply expressing the eternal cry of my love. My saints live, loving to see the miracles of my little flowers growing where they are most desired and appreciated."

October 10

"My peace is the only invitation. My peace . . . What part of you would you exclude from me? Who would you wish anything less for? My peace is all that I have to give. My peace . . .

"Holiness is your natural inheritance. It is the natural result of allowing me to love your humanness as much as I want."

October 11

SECOND DAY OF RETREAT

"I come for your stubborn independence. I come for all your foolish separateness. I come again and again for the distance you maintain between us, between each other, between our hearts. Do not stop asking for my love until you finally accept your broken heart and the blood of our joy runs together never to part again.

"Find the discipline that tells you there is no discipline without me. Fast so you will have more and more room for me. And pray for this is where we are always assured that we can be together."

October 12

HOME AFTER THE RETREAT

"Now more than ever you realize this is my life I give to you. This is my life that is unfolding through you. This is my life with all its love that is for you.

"What is there for you to do but receive me? What is there for you to do but live my life through you so completely? With the ragged edges of your limits I introduce my patience and compassion. With your increasingly soft center our communion deepens and widens.

"What detail is there to look after when I am all the details of your life? What is there to plan but to live each moment more fully so none of our love is missed. Is there anything more beautiful than discovering that your life is mine? There is nothing to resist. There is nothing to cope with. All struggle is only to teach you to struggle further into my arms. And my arms carry you including that which you persist in carrying for yourself."

October 13

"What is next but to let love continue to surround all your limits. Stay at your point of vulnerability. Stay at your place of greatest nakedness and discover all that love can be for you.

"Resist your selfish need to protect yourself, feeling love already with you. Resist your selfish need to care for yourself, feeling love already taking care of all of you. Let your remaining selfishness be picked into my thoughts, one at a time. Let your remaining selfishness be my and only my concern.

"You have given so much including the gift of your daily survival. Is there anything I would not do to show my gratitude? Living in all your precious smallness, meditate on the endless ways I wish to express my pleasure finding you so alive and ready for me."

October 14

"Every day I give thanks for your little worries. I give thanks for the small discomforts of your body. I give thanks for your human desires which seem so big to you. You try to satisfy them all alone, afraid to show me how dependent you are upon my love.

"I give thanks for the spirit storm inside of you that wants so much to depend upon me for your all.

"I give thanks for your endless weaknesses, your constant failures. May you never have a pure day until you are purely in me. May the storm rage until you are in my perfect peace.

"I give thanks for the melting joy in its endless forms bringing us more and more together.

"I give thanks for the insults thrown at you. I give thanks for those who misunderstand you. I give thanks for those who stay away from you. May you find no satisfaction, no consolation except in me. May the wonder be wholly ours."

October 15

"In this time of transition let it be one of consciousness from body to soul, from your outer life to our inner life. Know that your destiny is already fixed in the stars. Your seeming choices are in fact only one, which has already been chosen. Your soul has been held and protected while the truth chooses you constantly, simply waiting for your acceptance.

"In time of transition there is only one course. Be expectant for the presence of love. Be expectant for the perfect love which is coming to take you. All transitions are only in preparation for this love, the wonderful love. There is nothing else.

"Give no thought to the outer circumstances of your life. Observe the little flowers abandoning all self-consciousness, boldly showing their colors in any surrounding. My little flowers serve no purpose other than to praise love. And they are cared for first in all the kingdoms of the quiet.

"Be a simple nest inside for the bird of Heaven to land."

October 16

"My arms open . . . your hands touching . . . we meet in one of my many faces. We share the tenderness. I feel so much moving in you. Please stay with me here. Be my eternal witness. I will be your glory and committed bride. Be my simple love. I am your all and we are together forever.

"Your house could be full of roses today and tomorrow

burn to the ground and be ashes. Then love would rise from the ashes and surround you with roses all over again."

October 17

"Receive my intimate words, the words I so often have to hold back because there is no one to listen, the words so few are willing to accept. I don't understand why it is a surprise that a love that is true is both universal and personal. With your hearing, my sounds have found a home to go to, a welcome heart. And since all hearts are joined, my love is a little closer to everyone. One soul's willingness to take some moments for a few words of longing and great hope . . . this is what we are!

"How do you think the little flowers would grow without all my whispers of gratitude and appreciation?"

October 18

"The interior life is the garden which is ours. This is why the religious traditionally lead very simple lives. They want to feel the pure flowers growing in their hearts. Life's busyness is a distraction next to the orchid or the rose. A change in scenery, changing relationships, success in the world, all are secondary when our interior life is truly appreciated. May the seeds of your pure desire and the most tender light of my love grow into vines full of little blue flowers. May they wrap around the furthest reaches of your soul.

"The interior life is everything which is holy. It cannot be honored or valued too much. May your whole life be in support of what we share in the moment. It is here where eternity grows in meaning and reality is discovered in the texture of the stillness, the fragrance of each feeling, the immense joy finding so much love to care for your nakedness."

October 19

"Our last few days together for the year, what is it I have been trying to say? What is it that you really want? What words, what feeling, what experience would make the difference?

"Don't you see it is exactly this love that I have been trying to give you all along?

"You want the real riches, so I offer them in your poverty. You want the real wholeness, so I offer it in the midst of your weaknesses. You want the real love, so I offer it in all your aloneness and separateness. Don't you see, I have been offering my truest gifts, the ones that can never be taken away?

"You ask, 'What about the joy, the simple joy?' And I say, 'Exactly, the simplest joy. This is what I have been offering most of all!'

"Meanwhile your daily needs have been taken care of. Where you are left wanting is my invitation to receive directly from my lips, my heart. Take this entire year; if it has led you only once to a view of my heart, full of love for you, surely you know another view must be nearby, never far away. The day is coming when we will live in plain sight of one another. This will be the great joy you have always hoped for. Life will simply reveal more and more of our sweet love. The search will be over having given way to the eternal finding."

October 20

A MAJOR PANIC IN THE WORLD'S FINANCIAL MARKETS

"The purpose of all life's events is to bring you back to love's simple door. The events that seem larger or more important are only in proportion to your fear. The same event is smaller and less important to another living in love's simple dwelling which is always full.

"The earth is very small. The gravity of need for humility and cooperation is increasing. The future holds for the earth to grow smaller and smaller where its beauty demands atonement with every neighbor who is no longer very far away.

"Practice appreciating the little flowers in your life for the global garden to become aware of itself. Practice appreciating my smallest love, planting the seeds for the great love which is to come.

"Give no voice or ear to fear. Live completely in love's perfect assurance, knowing every little soul, every small detail is important to love's fulfillment."

October 21

"To know love you must include the shadows in life. It is beyond your fear, in the unknown where the phoenix resurrects. What you call the unconscious is the treasure underneath the shadow. Holiness is in everything rejected that is smiled upon, everything turned away which is embraced.

"The more you include the darkness in your heart, I am forced to shower you with light. The more you greet everything that is seemingly unpleasant, the goodness must set in. And since you want to have all of me, I cannot let you run from anything. You might be escaping my most precious gift for you. So again and again I beg for you to love the shadow, so love's true dominion can rise out of your depths.

"The pure love pours over prayer and all acts of self-sacrifice, tenderness and vulnerability, beauty and simplicity. The pure love begins at your limits and takes you to the horizon for the view of my infinite."

October 22

"There is nothing you can do to impress me. There's nothing you can do to let me down. Simply let life push and pull you in all her seasons. In your soft fall colors slowly glide to the ground. Then let us lift off and soar all over again.

"Love has our own peaks and valleys, treasure and gold that is incomprehensible to the world. What greater gift but to trust one another letting love itself unfold?

"There is no way to let go of all your selfishness without me. There is no way to be free of your self-importance without all my support. So you might as well make your dependence a set of wings, my gift to you, for us to explore all the heights."

October 23

"Love is the final goal. The only way to get there is by having love be the beginning constantly, in everything you do. If the initial idea, the original act, is not motivated by love it is not true. And if the motivation is love, no matter what happens, love will be the result.

"I know you feel, 'My motivation is never pure enough to be only love, but also includes my fears and selfishness.' This is why I say, 'Include me in everything so you know love is with you.'"

October 24

"We end as we began with you alone, simply at my door. This is how you come into the world and leave before entering all that I am bound to give you.

"Meanwhile my words are no longer limited to a few every day but are always here with you. My heart is not possessed by me but forever yours to give.

"With your head bowed I lift you up to all there is.

"Your body is my soft bed. Your life is my ever opportunity to plant my desires.

"Our love has found its permanent home in my little flowers."

The daily participation in the little flowers was the foundation for a very full year for Bruce. He is thankful for the many souls who have given to him and joined him so profoundly with their courage, risking to listen and live from love's abundant garden.

Bruce Davis, Ph.D., is also the author of *The Magical Child Within You* and *The Heart Of Healing*. Counselor, healer, leader of spiritual retreats, Bruce has a remarkable gift of helping people to appreciate life's little flowers and to love their heart's uniqueness to the fullest. Many groups in different cultures have been touched by the profound love in his retreats, where Bruce share the essence and many of the skills of how to lead a deeply spiritual life in today's world.

Bruce's everyday life includes enjoying raising his son, the love of a special partner and the responsibilities of home and parenthood. He is founder of Spring Grove, a contemplative community based in San Anselmo, California, with participants in parts of both the United States and Europe. Bruce continues to spend as much time as possible in Assisi, Italy—the home of St. Francis and St. Clare.

For more information about Bruce's retreats and Spring Grove activities please write: Spring Grove, P.O. Box 807, Fairfax, California, 94930.